Rocket Your Nonprofit

Accelerate Your Mission & Impact, Eliminate Obstacles & Feeling Overwhelmed

Carrie Reichartz

Copyright © 2023 by Carrie Reichartz
All rights reserved.
ISBN: 9780985945695

Infinitely More Life Publishing

TABLE OF CONTENTS

Introduction: Stepping Into God's Calling For You 5

Chapter 1: Vision Begins: Pain, Purpose, Passion & Prayer 15

Chapter 2: God's Got The Power… But Who's In Charge? 25

Chapter 3: Foundation Under Construction: Character (Self Leadership)..37

Chapter 4: Start Small: Keep Going...49

Chapter 5: There's Purpose In The Process: Embracing & Releasing 61

Chapter 6:	Where Are The Battlefields: Will You Keep Going?	71
Chapter 7:	Fighting Back	79
Chapter 8:	Set It And Forget It Funding: Overcoming Fear Of Funding	89
Chapter 9:	People: Money Is Not The Most Important Provision	101
Chapter 10:	Trusting, Leading, & Finding Your People	111
Chapter 11:	Mercy's Miracles Moments: Lessons From Along The Way	121
Chapter 12:	Where Do We Go From Here?	137

INTRODUCTION
STEPPING INTO GOD'S CALLING FOR YOU

A God-given dream had become a reality and we were standing in the midst of it! In May 2018, Mercy's Light Family opened its doors after a 10-year faith journey and finally it was visible! Long-time Kenyan and American friends and partners gathered together for a housewarming party. Laughter filled the mustard yellow colored dining room and bright green playroom as we celebrated together.

In between the conversations, reminiscent speeches and drinking sweet passion fruit juice, God whispered to me as I was passing out cake:

> "Write down the journey of raising up this nonprofit with me and share it with others."

Though I did not realize it, that whisper, in the midst of a large, celebrating crowd, launched the next step in my journey with God: Christian Rocketeers, a new movement to rocket other nonprofits around the world and in the US. In that busy, joy-filled moment, on this long-awaited day, there was already a subtle, but powerful call to do something more!

Once I heard God so clearly, I knew I couldn't ignore this call, but I was slow to take action at first. The vision and mission of Mercy's Light - ending and healing sex trafficking and financial empowerment of pregnant teens and their babies- was big. How could I possibly take on more?

But then I read Acts 10:34-38 NIV:

> ..Peter began to speak: "I now realize how true it is that God does not show favoritism **35** but accepts from every nation the one who fears him and does what is right. **36** You know the message God sent to the people of Israel, announcing the good news of peace through Jesus Christ, who is Lord of all....**38** ...God anointed Jesus of Nazareth with the Holy Spirit and power, ...he went around doing good and healing all who were under the power of the devil, because God was with him...

I knew God would give me the power to do whatever He called me to. He will do the same for you! He, with our cooperation, makes us shine like the stars He created us to be stars that bring hope to the hopeless and love to the loveless. Our ability to shine, if we connect it with His truth and vision for our lives, is limitless! Unstoppable! We just have to say "yes". I said yes, will you?

WHO AM I?

Hi, I'm Carrie Reichartz, Chief Rocket Launcher of the Christian Rocketeers movement. This wasn't always my role. My life and career were radically transformed 12 years earlier by encountering the powerful love of God in Kenya on a short-term mission trip.

God interrupted my plans. I had a fulfilling career climbing the corporate ladder as a lawyer. Shortly after being nominated by my lawyer peers, I received the honor of the *Rising Star lawyer* award! All the years of hard work, expensive education, were paying off. But there was a missing piece inside of me that I thought these achievements and accomplishments would fill, and it was even bigger than it was when I started law school.

In the midst of this internal unrest God called me to Kenya. He exposed desperate needs: kids starving to death, living in mud huts, walking 3 miles per day to reach water for all the household needs, (and therefore unable to go to school). I was overwhelmed by the deep need that surrounded me.

God called me to leave my legal career behind and open a small home business. I left the financially secure and comfortable employee life making: $175/**hour** to start making $175/**week** for **50-60 hours** in a home childcare running my own business and relying on Him. I went from having the clout of status and title of being a lawyer to being a babysitter. I left my reputation in His hands.

Though the transition was difficult for me, my new husband and our blended family with preteen kids, it was incredibly rewarding! It was less money, but more time together. Our kids didn't always see it as a blessing!

My new lifestyle left me time and mental energy to make a difference for my kids, who had recently lost their dad to a heroin addiction, and for the kids and missionaries in Kenya. With God's help, every day I started fighting against systemic spiritual, emotional, and financial poverty around the world. First through Operation Give Hope (OGH), the first nonprofit I established with Jim Horne, a missionary pastor and others in Mombasa, Kenya.

We reached over 1,200 children, plus adults, each day with life changing transformation. Under God's direction, OGH created schools, Bible colleges, local churches, feeding centers, medical centers, rescue centers, general community outreaches and most importantly touched a people group unreached by the Gospel with His loving touch and His Word.

People also approached me asking for help using my legal skills to start nonprofits God was calling them to. In 2010, I started helping others with the legal paperwork, specializing in international nonprofits. I could see the depth and breadth of need in the world everyday.

The piece that was missing climbing the corporate ladder was found - living out what Jesus put me on the earth to do! (Ephesians 2:10)

MY NONPROFIT JOURNEY: MERCY'S LIGHT FAMILY (MLF)

While doing all this legal nonprofit work on the side, I continued to travel to Kenya 2-3 times per year and continued to run my small childcare business. Through many tough circumstances, God slowly revealed how He had uniquely prepared my life for a certain assignment: "Giving a voice" to young girls who suffer emotional and sexual trauma (trafficking, rape, sexual abuse) around the world and become pregnant.

My own personal past history of rape and sexual abuse as well as early pregnancy, uniquely equipped me in certain areas. My lack of education or experience in raising funds, running a large organization, or any nonlegal area of nonprofits, left me scared and overwhelmed.

I did not know what to do or where to start. There was nothing similar in Kenya. I had no extra personal financial resources and my business and social circle was not excited about supporting Christian work overseas.

I tried reaching out to the secular sources of nonprofit support and they left me overwhelmed with a laundry list of 1,000 things I HAD to do if I wanted to be successful. I had no possible way of accomplishing them. I was overwhelmed by anxiety, fear, and excuses. I spent many years stuck there and many babies and young girls suffered because of it.

Though it wasn't easy or pretty, God led me through the process and that was FINALLY coming to fruition that day in May 2018; 10 years after I first arrived in Kenya.

SOMETHING NEW, AN INVITATION

Now at this monumental moment, God was whispering something new. He used this moment at the housewarming party in Kenya to lead me to my next phase of purpose: equipping, coaching and creating CHRISTIAN nonprofit leaders.

*He wants you to avoid pitfalls, many of which I fell into along the way.

*He wants you to know you are not alone on the journey, like I felt I was for most of it.

*He wants Christian nonprofits sky-rocketing to quick success in Him - not in ourselves or the world's way.

God wants this done and He has invited me to lead the way using the experiences He took me through in starting Mercy's Light Family!

Ok, if I'm honest, it took me a while to get onboard with this whole Christian Rocketeers thing. I didn't even like the name He gave us. This book took 4 years to write. I love the work I do with Mercy's Light and the family of donors, volunteers and staff we have there.

What finally pushed me over the edge were three things: first - two dreams He gave me of wheat fields ready for harvest and me being the only one there to do all the work; second - a deep "why" from within my soul to see God's work spread throughout the earth in our Christian nonprofit clients; and third - to see His shining star children leading nonprofits and living every day in His will and purpose with ease and grace, not strife and anxiety!

This book is not necessarily a "how to". Our courses, community, and coaching cover our process in exact easy to follow steps. It's an example of all that God can and WILL do if you let Him in your life. It is an invitation….

Invitation to see the ripple effect of what one person being obedient to God can accomplish.

Invitation to shine! To learn how to shine for Him!

Invitation to be a part of something bigger than yourself.

Invitation to EXPERIENCE that God has no limit! Jesus states in the Word, "We will do greater things than Him!" (John 14:12 NIV) Will you let Him prove that?

SUCH A TIME AS THIS

Lives of young girls and babies were being lost as I was dragging my feet to fully start this nonprofit mission. Lives are probably suffering and being lost as you wait to start the vision and mission God has for YOUR life.

God created you for such a time as this. He had your exact purpose in mind when He knit you together in your mother's womb and placed you on this earth! You are not meant to get up and go to work and come home and watch Netflix, play phone games, and social media. Don't wait another minute to step into the purpose He has for your life!

God hasn't called others to serve where and how He has called YOU! Don't miss out on that. Even more, don't let the people you are called to reach miss out on His love, help, and healing because you aren't taking the action He is calling you to. Remember, others are waiting for you. Join the journey with the Christian Rocketeers as we venture together to build His Kingdom in this world! Let's stop the suffering together or whatever He is calling you to!

For me, it started with a Mercy's Light Family vision and mission, and then the call and invitation (that looked like an interruption) to take it to the next level to help others start Christian nonprofits with Christian Rocketeers. I felt scared, anxious and overwhelmed just like you do. God is calling you to take it to the next level with Him and He is providing you with Christian Rocketeers to help you! Let's learn to build, grow and partner with God as you launch your own vision and mission from God!

Please hear me. Anyone God has called CAN do this! If God has called you, you are able! He has made you. You have everything you need to make this happen. Trust Him! Until you can fully trust Him, trust me! I felt the same way you do right now.

God does not call the equipped, He equips the called.

Moses didn't ask to be picked to rescue the Israelites from Egypt, but God prepared Him his whole life for the task and provided all the finances and everything else needed. Moses (in Exodus 3) doubted and yet God used Him. Why? Because Moses was willing to let Him. He was an ordinary person, doing ordinary things, and when God called him to greater things. Despite his own fears and self-identified inadequacies. The same God that used a reluctant Moses to do great things has a plan to use you! The only question mark is will you let Him?

MERCY'S LIGHT FAMILY JOURNEY

As for my Mercy's Light Family nonprofit journey so far, we are the first center of its kind on the north coast of Mombasa, rescuing young moms and raising them together with their babies, healing sexual trauma and leading moms to self-sufficiency through employment and business. We started from nowhere, raising it up from beneath the surface. We had no special connections, no massive financing, no policies and procedures, no system to copy. We had nothing.

Now just four years later, through the 3-year program that God downloaded to us for His work in Kenya, 50+ girls and babies have been rescued from sex trafficking or trauma and the dire poverty they endured their whole lives. They have been placed for employment, sent back to school if they have safe families, or started their own businesses to support themselves and their babies!

Our staff love their extremely difficult work. When we went to Him to learn how to hire, we haven't had any turnover in the last 3.5 years! In fact, staff often say they should pay us to work there. They get so much out of their service.

There has been miraculous life transforming results for girls, babies, and staff. Miracle after miracle! We have gotten positive government attention, large organizations are approaching us wanting to partner, and other missions are wanting our help to improve their programs to increase results!

Whatever nonprofit mission God is calling you to do, our Christian Rocketeers framework will work for you. It is not about our specific 3-year program (though we are happy to share that with you). This is about ending homelessness in the United States; healing of children in foster care; ministering to the needs of special needs families; starting a Bible College around the world. It is about whatever He is burdening you with and calling you to and equipping you to take the next right steps in doing that!

Christian Rocketeers has equipped hundreds of nonprofit leaders and founders to rocket past fear and excuses to serve the clients God called them to. They got to skip 12 years of trouble, heartache, financial stress to skyrock to quicker success in start up, funding, growing, scaling and leading a successful Christian nonprofit. Over one million children and adults across the globe have been impacted, imparted, influenced, and inspired through a year with us and our clients! Maybe you will be next.

Or will you, like I did at first, let excuses, justification, fear, lack of people and finances stop you from making a kingdom impact?

WHAT IS A CHRISTIAN ROCKETEER?

Wondering what exactly is a Christian Rocketeer? Check out our manifesto - just a fancy word for what we believe and what we don't believe and how we live!

You're invited on a journey to being the next Christian Rocketeer! Don't worry about whatever may come up along the way. You won't be taking this journey alone. You will be partnering with God. Remember, He created this universe, you and your purpose and all the funding and people needed to make it happen.

After this journey, you may decide to link arms with us and our expert guidance, instruction, and invaluable resources to turn your nonprofit dreams/vision into reality to stop the suffering for the people He is calling you to serve with ease and grace!

Whatever you decide, I want you to let go of YOU. (What you think you can do, what you think is possible.) I want you to embrace all that God can and will do through you if you let Him! He is faithful and He will show up. Trust Him.

My hope is this book will impact you! It will INSPIRE you to act on YOUR God-given life purpose. Leading you to impart and influence others. Stop letting fear of being overwhelmed win. Let's start shining His love into the world! This book will take you on a mission to see His power. We will see that power at work through Biblical examples and a current real life example of my life.

I invite you to travel back in time with me, to journey through my story. Are you ready? Let's start at the beginning….

CHAPTER 1
VISION BEGINS: PAIN, PURPOSE, PASSION & PRAYER

This journey to the nonprofit mission God has called you comes from Him. It is revealed through your time with Him and prayer. Though there are exceptions, it usually comes from a deep emotional pain (empathy) in our life. God heals that pain and redeems it by turning it into a passion and purpose which ushers us to vision and mission. Vision and mission shines brightest from deepest pain - our own and others.

When I think about a life filled with vision and mission coming from great pain, passion, and purpose, I think of the story of Joseph. He was sold into slavery by his own brothers, betrayed and wrongly accused of sexual allegations by his boss' wife, imprisoned and abandoned. He experienced great pain. Yet, despite all this pain, he did not become bitter. Joseph stayed focused on God and because of that he saved his whole family and the nation of Israel from starvation, got married, had children, and was very wealthy. (See Genesis 37-50.)

Reading Joseph's story, you can see he had no idea what his purpose was through his suffering; but once God got him to the palace, a place Joseph was not seeking, all the suffering experiences made him an amazing leader and he had great vision for the mission God called Him to lead. Vision and mission are formed in the midst of pain, passion, purpose and prayer. Let's see how pain can transform into vision and mission.

PAIN

Pain is a rocket that carries us. It drives us either closer to Christ or further away from Him. Christ does not cause or create the pain, a fallen world does that. He *promises* to redeem it; but we must bring it to Him.

In his pain, Joseph allowed Christ to stay at the forefront of his life and his pain was redeemed. If Joseph would have chosen bitterness and anger; then his pain would have been wasted instead of redeemed by God.

Think of redemption like redeeming a coupon. You don't get to take the coupon back with you after you redeem it. You HAVE to leave it BEHIND. That's exactly what Joseph did. He focused on God and what was before him and left his pain with God.

As we allow God to come in and heal our pain by simply surrendering it to Him, He redeems the pain.

Romans 8:28 NIV:

> And we know that *in all things* God works for the good of those who love Him, who have been called according to his purpose.

Not He works just the good and fun for our good, but IN ALL THINGS. If I love Him and allow myself to be called into HIS purpose, He works for MY good!

Jesus will "shine" through our painful stories if we allow ourselves to be vulnerable and share our pain with Him and others. As we do that, we develop passion.

PASSION

If pain is a rocket, passion is a deep feeling that gets and keeps the rocket moving forward. It's the rocket fuel that ignites a fire, motivating us out of our comfort zones.

Our pain produces motivation to "do something"! That is passion. For Joseph that passion showed through his diligent work at the house and in prison despite the unfair circumstances that brought him there. It also shined through his dream interpretation which later led to his appearance before the Pharaoh. How did Joseph do it? He kept his focus on God and not the painful circumstances around him.

While I sat comfortably in my suburban home leading my life - work, kids, TV, computer games, social media, etc - babies were being aborted and abandoned out of desperation in Kenya. Girls were being left abandoned, alone and afraid in the streets after experiencing sexual trauma. Trauma I could relate to. Without passion, we sit complacent in our comfortable and secure lives while others are deeply hurting. We are also hurting deeply in depression and anxiety as well. We need to keep focused on God and His grand purpose for our lives to keep ourselves out of anxiety and depression and to live out the amazing life His son died to give us!

CHRIST'S PASSION EXAMPLE

Christ's walk to the cross is called "the passion" and is a great example of what I'm talking about here. He sweated blood hoping to find another way other than the cross. When there was none. His passionate love for us led Him straight into enduring immense emotional, physical and spiritual pain. Because of His passion for us, He resolved to walk those painful steps. How did He do it? He kept His focus on His Father and us.

Passion is like a rocket being launched to the moon. There will be moments of pure delight and excitement and there will be moments of fear and uncertainty.

Passion has some emotional messiness for a while. If you're like me, that is really uncomfortable. I prefer to keep it all together, publicly at least. God's Word tells us that His power is made perfect in our weakness, not our strength (2 Corinthians 12:9). As you are open, the heavens will be open to you! That means vision, finances, people and whatever you need to walk out what He is calling you to. I know this from experience!

Passion, and the emotion behind it, leads us to do things that we cannot do in our human strength, and say things we didn't think we could say. Things only God can do through us. Passion will keep you focused on the end goal of your nonprofit mission - keeping focused on God and easing the suffering for the people He has called you to serve - no matter the circumstances around you. This intense focus will walk us right into the purpose He has for you!

PURPOSE

If pain is our rocket and passion is our fuel, then purpose is our destination! Like a rocket, landing is not always precise!

God's Word defines purpose in Ephesians 2:10:

> For we are God's handiwork, created in Christ Jesus to do good works, which God prepared in advance for us to do.

This verse immediately takes the pressure off of us! He created us for a purpose. We don't need to create it, find it, figure it out, manufacture it, make it happen, or anything else. He has taken care of all the details. He prepared these things in advance. All we need to do is connect and walk it out.

Purpose is a combination of all your life experiences (good and difficult), abilities and gifts He gives you. Mix that with the specifics He shares in His Word: love, forgiveness and service. As you spend time focused on Him, He will add His "super" to your "natural", all mixed together creating something SUPERNATURAL!

Purpose will always lead back to loving Him and seeking Him with our full hearts. Anything that takes you away from Him is not your purpose.*

Carrie Reichartz

VISION & MISSION

As passion takes root through prayer and focused attention with God, we will talk about that more specifically below. As passion takes a deeper root, it turns to vision and mission; leading to action. At the beginning, like with Joseph it won't always be clear. But, as you take baby steps into opportunities He puts before you, even when it doesn't make sense, and it's scary and sometimes hurts, your vision and mission will become more clear.

Vision and mission are usually birthed out of personal experiences with pain. Let's spend a bit of time digging into your story. Below are a few writing prompts for you. Take 10 minutes to write out your answers to all three of these questions. Pray and ask God to reveal more to you.

What is your personal story with deep pain?

How have you been deeply impacted by someone else's pain?

Are you deeply hurt by an issue or circumstance?

These deep pain points develop into passion and purpose. From there God will reveal the specific vision and mission He wants your nonprofit to tackle.

If you wrote out your story above and no emotion came with it, keep writing or find another topic because this one wasn't deep enough to carry you through. You will encounter difficulties on this nonprofit journey. Make sure your pain, passion and purpose are deep enough!

For me - it was deep sadness over all I had lost in my life, the excruciating fear I lived in daily without even realizing it. Maybe it's the same for you. Or maybe it's deep-seeded anger. Whatever it is for you, let the emotion come up and out.

Now let's dive deeper into our pain, passion, purpose, and prayer.

TOOLS TO TURN PAIN TO PURPOSE

These tools are helpful in turning your pain into vision and mission. You will see some of these tools come up again and again in our journey together. Each time we will go deeper and use them for various purposes.

To be a successful leader of anything we need to have our spiritual life in order. It is from this all things in life flow.

1. Personal Prayer & Bible Study Time

Are you looking for a lighted path on your nonprofit journey? "Your word is a lamp for my feet, a light on my path." Psalm 119:105 NIV

The main bridge between pain and passion is the Word of God and prayer. Daily time with His truth transformed my emotions and my life. At first I would open the Word and not understand what I was reading. Most of it didn't make sense and the devil distracted me. It was hard to make myself sit down and do it.

In fact, the first time I read through the Bible it took me a year and a half. I got very little from it, other than being able to say I read it. But, through the process, I found writing out the scripture verses slowed me down to actually try to understand what I was reading. I still didn't understand most of it. I learned to focus on the words that would rise off the page at me and, as I focused on those verses, He showed me things in my life that the verse applied to.

Once I made the commitment to read through the Bible in one year, showing up for 20 minutes per morning, five days per week, things started changing. Slowly, I started seeing results in my thoughts and actions. As I moved past the struggle of *making* time for the Word, I moved into hungering and thirsting for the Word. The more you're in the Word the more it changes you and the more you want it.

I could see, and those around me could see, my emotions, actions and thoughts transforming: my marriage was more peaceful; parenting was easier; life had more joy and was becoming easier. Romans 12:1-2 was showing itself in my life. Slowly things were changing! Pain was turning into passion and purpose.

I was praying and asking Him to reveal Himself more and lead my life. He does that through His Word and quiet time as we wait on Him. We will talk more about this in our writing and future chapters.

MAKING PERSONAL BIBLE STUDY TIME EFFECTIVE: HAVE A PLAN

Having a plan in place of what you will read is key to success. Don't try to figure it out each morning as you go, have it set. You should have a specific reading plan for your personal time. Follow it. If you're not sure, hop online and search "read through the Bible in a year" plan and get started with personal time with God. It's more about being in the Word than having a specific plan.

Also, have a specific time and place you do this personal devotional work. Have everything you need in that space - pens, paper, Bible, and photos for encouragement. The place can be a chair in the living room, a table in your closet, your kitchen table with a basket full of your supplies that you bring with you. Make sure you have a certain place and time you meet Jesus for "date time" every day.

It will transform your life! Don't miss out on all the God has for you in this precious time!

2. Church & Involvement: Christian Fellowship

Regular attendance in church is another key to keeping you on the right path with Christ and leading you into his purpose, vision and mission for your life. Church and Christian community is key. Don't miss out. Regular church attendance at a local body of believers is critical. Don't let yourself be deceived into thinking otherwise. Hebrews 10:24-25 (NKJV) says:

> And let us consider one another in order to stir up love and good works, not forsaking the assembling of ourselves together, as *is* the manner of some, but exhorting *one another,* and so much the more as you see the Day approaching.

This meeting together is especially important when we go through tough times. When things were the darkest and when EVERYTHING seemed to be going wrong, the sermon and/or worship songs at my church touched my pain. I remember when my children's father passed away, and being new to church. I just sat crying and crying through the songs and sermons and felt the love of Christ around me even though I didn't know anyone.

God uses the local church to support us, give us strength, encouragement, refreshment and, at times, convict us. Regular church attendance at the same place of worship is critical to knowing and living God's purpose, vision and mission for your life.

3. Group Bible Studies

Are you in a regular group Bible study that is studying the Word of God in depth in a small circle or on zoom? Group Bible studies are important to keep you accountable to being in the Word, in addition to your own personal quiet time.

It is important that you can be humble, open, and transparent in your group. If you are not willing to open up and be honest, Christ's sacrifice will be lost on you.

If you don't have a group that you can be that open in yet, keep looking. There is a group for you out there. Check your church and other churches in your area. BSFinternational.org has amazing studies, in person and online. You can also check out our Christian Rocketeers Facebook page; we also host Bible studies for nonprofit leaders.

Wherever you decide to jump in; be all in. Be committed, show up and do the homework. Be humble, open and transparent and encourage others in your group to do the same as well.

It was during my darkest times - when I couldn't go minutes without crying because my heart hurt so bad - when I was so confused and didn't know what to do next - that my Bible study groups poured into me. Because I had been honest and open, sharing the awesome times I had with God and also sharing the hurt and the pain I was currently in, they could remind me of all God had done in His Word and in my life previously. They helped me remember how loved I was. They prayed over me. They reminded me of where to keep my eyes in dark times. They kept me grounded in the Word.

4. **Writing/Journaling**

Let me be clear - I hate to journal! I have horrible handwriting. It takes too much time; however I know, when I choose to do it anyway, I am always closer to God and my purpose than before I pick up the pen and paper! Writing cleans and clarifies our soul. He brings healing to pain and clarity to purpose through writing. The examples of this could be endless, but here is one:

In 2012, I was not sure I would EVER head back to Kenya again. There was a dramatic exit from a meeting by my then partner that left me reeling the whole plane ride home where I was greeted by an unexpected negative email from my other partner.

During that traumatic time, God used a dear friend, Charlie Evans, to lead me to write about my Kenyan journeys so far. After reviewing blog posts, photos and journals God brought forth to me I wrote *From Lawyer To Missionary: A Journey to Kenya and Back Again* in just one week. A book that continues to get rave reviews for the honest "take you along for the journey" look back at all my trips to Kenya.

Through that writing, God revealed the clarity I needed to determine what next steps in Kenya would be. Taking the 30,000 foot view of ALL the conversations I had with government officials to village women through the entire journey, He revealed His purpose to me.

I could not see that clarity in the middle of it. I only saw unmet needs and a mess. Through my writing, He brought clarity. Writing is an important piece of your nonprofit journey. Writing your personal story, the nonprofit journey, stories of those you touch and more. Writing is needed for vision and mission clarity and also to effectively share all stories of the nonprofit with your donors and potential donors. Make it a daily habit.

PAIN, PASSION & PURPOSE ARE NOT ENOUGH

We have experienced deep hurts in various ways in our lives. Deep hurts and needs exist in people in this world. He created you in a unique way. Your life experiences and exposures perfectly equip you to meet other needs. Are you willing to leave people suffering because you are overwhelmed and not sure where to start or because you are afraid? I hope not. You can do this! Let's get started on His vision and mission for your life!

Pain, passion and purpose are great foundational elements to get started, but they are not enough to sustain vision and mission. To do that, we need power. Let's dive into that next.

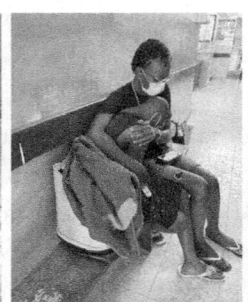

CHAPTER 2
GOD'S GOT THE POWER...
BUT WHO'S IN CHARGE?

This is too big! I hear this from our clients all the time. The vision alone is way too big for me to handle. Add to that, being worried about money, people and things that we didn't have. I was attempting to do 12 fundraisers a year to desperately bring in funds. I was also taking every meeting with anyone in hopes it might lead to something. Throughout all this, I was not involving God in the process.

I thought Mercy's Light would grow if:

*I was busy enough.
*I tried harder and longer.
*I achieved enough.
*I had enough education.
*I analyzed the problem enough.
*I had more money.
*I had enough donors and volunteers.

Then He would reward me. Then everything would be perfect.

I told myself that if I did all these things, then my ministry would be successful. I would have all the money and people I needed. I attended Christian nonprofit conferences that cemented these thoughts.

Doing things this way for years caused burnout, exhaustion, and lack of time for family and friends. It got me nowhere fast as I cycled through overwhelm and anxiety. I was trying to push forward; but instead I was only circling like the Isrealites in the wilderness and was exhausted.

After many years of ministry, I have seen some success, no success and tremendous success. I am here to tell you none of the above things will make your ministry successful. Where does the power and drive come from for our ministries? Let's explore that together.

HOW ARE MINISTRIES BUILT?

Ministries that are built to last are built in the secret, quiet space time with God; spending regular and focused time in relationship with Him and asking, seeking and knocking for personal needs, clarity, next steps of vision and yes, even provision (Matthew 7:7). To build a solid and profitable ministry and to be able to do all the things He has called us to, first we need to seek the Lord. Boldly and confidently approaching Him (Ephesian 3:12).

To truly seek Him, we need to be in His Word. There is no excuse not to be in His Word. He came to the Earth for us, and He left His Word for us. We need to seek that like we seek life. As we do, He speaks to us about our current circumstances through His Word.

He is bigger than His Word. We have the Holy Spirit alive and active in us! However, the devil is also equally active in this world and, if we are not seeking His Word daily, we won't know enough about Him to know the difference between Him and the devil. The devil can offer us some pretty amazing opportunities and if we are not in the Word and seeking Him, we will be led astray. Be consistently in the physical part He has left for us to seek.

God's Word is clear on how we are to live - love, forgive, be humble - are a few examples. Are we doing those things? If not, we start there. As we become consistent in these things, He will open the doors to next opportunities to serve with Him.

Second, we need to inquire of Him and have specific time we spend asking the right questions and LISTENING for answers.

"Lord teach me more about you."
"How can I be more like Your son today?"
"Lord, teach me Your ways?
"Lord, what do you want from me? Where can I serve? What can I do?"

Keep your focus on Him and He will reveal all things to you. (Jeremiah 33:3)

From there we move to ministry questions like:

Which fundraisers to host or relationships to pursue? More important - which ones to let go of?
Where to find volunteers and donors?
And all other questions you have.

Create space in your life to listen for the answers. As you devote time to journal the answers to your specific questions, you will hear from Him.

As you continue this process you want to constantly be checking, "Are we seeking Him and not just what we want from Him? That's a hard line when you need money NOW to support projects He has called you to. I'm sitting in that exact position right now as I write.

If He has called you to a project, it is His project to fund and support not yours. Don't step in and help Him. He doesn't need your help and you will end up overwhelmed. I know it's not easy as you start, but it works and He works in perfect timing. Trust Him!

To be able to do this well and long term, you need to put some mental health checks in place to keep your focus on Him and not you.

MENTAL HEALTH CHECK: REMEMBER, IT ONLY TAKES SOMETHING SMALL FROM GOD TO CHANGE A WHOLE COMMUNITY

There is a process to this nonprofit journey. Strong mental health and nonprofit health is found in letting go of our personal thoughts, ideas, actions. Instead, focus on adopting His will, ideas, and actions. Stop living in the "what I can do, control, analyze, achieve, what makes sense, what do the experts do" list and move to living in the power of the Holy Spirit.

For your mental health you need to keep a few things at the forefront of your mind. First, He loves you as much as He possibly can now; project or no project; money or no money; people or no people.

Nothing you ever will do or say will get Him to love you more or less.

Even in our mess ups, He loves.

Even in our greatest failures and darkest emotional moments, He loves us.

The success, or even failure, of this project will not in any way affect His love for you. He doesn't NEED you to do this project. He is inviting you on a journey with Him. What he desires is a relationship with you. He is using this project as one way to do that.

Will you trust Him enough to follow His thoughts and not your own?

Second, this is not about you. It's about Him and sharing Him with others.

He laid down His life for ours the day He went to the cross to defeat sin and the devil for us. Every day we have a chance to lay down our rights for Him, on behalf of others, to show them a living example of who He is. Are you willing to lay down your rights to fight for the rights of others?

REAL LIFE EXAMPLE

When I started this journey with Him in 2008, I was begging Him to share what He wanted my vision and mission to be for Kenya. Why was He calling me to Kenya over and over again? I wanted to know what exactly He wanted me to do so I could get it done for Him. He seemed to be remaining silent. Can you relate?

The problem was I was asking the wrong question. I was asking what MY mission was. I should have been asking: "Lord, what is Your mission here in Kenya and how would you like me to help?"

Even though I wasn't asking the right questions, the Lord put something small before me, something I didn't feel would work. This "something" wasn't enough to solve the problem He was putting before me, but He gave me an opportunity to trust Him.

START A BIBLE STUDY…

Sweaty and exhausted emotionally, spiritually, physically, and mentally after a long day of ministry to the women in Kenya, my friend Sue and I didn't know what to do. We were child care business owners and shared about being ambassadors for Christ and asked advice about how to discipline their children. We shared our advice: make sure they get plenty of sleep, get to bed early and naps.

Their response back to us was gracious. They followed up with questions like:

"When we put them to bed, they rock back and forth all night because they are hungry and I have no food to feed them."

UGH…. what? I cannot even imagine… the tears well up in my eyes.

Then they asked: "Is it ok to leave my kids home alone at night so I can go out to the streets and make some money to feed them?"

How can I even begin to imagine the pain these women and their babies are going through? Sue and I pointed them back to the Word of God and prayer and remarkably the ladies seemed to leave energized. But, when we came back home, we were tearful and defeated feeling like we didn't have any answers.

As much as we wanted to and wished we could, we could not make a difference in the physical reality of these women or their children.

We were feeling overwhelmed and hurting for these beautiful women, God laid an idea on our hearts: start a Bible study.

While my heart was aching for these moms, it didn't seem enough. How was it going to make a bit of a difference in the physical reality of these ladies and their children? But, because of His leading, we tried it.

As we prayed, Nicole, a teacher at an Operation Give Hope school came to mind to lead that study in Vipingo. She was reluctant because being younger, culturally, she didn't feel comfortable in a role of leadership.

She agreed to try it if we sent her materials.

One year later, when we arrived, she was preaching like a pastor on a Sunday morning with power, poise and grace without notes. It was a beautiful thing to see!

Now 35+ women regularly attend Bible studies, community outreaches, days of prayer and fasting, and they host women's conferences!

Just a short time ago I learned that because of this group's conferences other Bible study groups are spurring off. Those groups are also starting to host Christian Women's conferences all over the area during the year as well! Remember this is an area unreached by the Gospel. Praise God!

The women are now happier, more of their needs are being met by their walk with God and the local church. I don't know the specifics of the women that asked the original questions, but I do know God is moving and changing lives spiritually, physically, emotionally, and mentally all around Vipingo.

His one thing was enough! Just because we allowed his thoughts (start a Bible study) to direct our actions, now that Bible study is also pouring into our girls and staff at Mercy's Light Family.

We had no idea when we started the Bible study all that God would do and continue to do through it. But God knew...and He worked out all the details.

As I let go of control and did what He was calling in the moment, He worked out the details. I was obedient and He took care of the rest.

As I sit here typing this, today, God is leading us to more and bigger things in Vipingo. I sometimes question myself and the finances; but, as I look back on all the times He's provided for us, I know He can and I know He will do it again, as long as I stay out of the way.

What do we do in the meantime? How do we trust God when it doesn't look possible? It requires remembering the Bible's history of Him, remembering your history with Him, and trusting Him until the promise He made comes true!

HOW TO ACCESS & STAY IN HIS POWER AND NOT OURS

To run a mission that will carry out His purposes, we will need direction and power from Him! Let me share a few of the ways He has taught me to stay connected with Him and His power.

1. Remembering His History in His Word

Through 2 Peter 1:3, God shares how we access His divine power.

> *"**His divine power** has given us everything we need for a godly life **through our knowledge of him** who called us by his own glory and goodness."*

Did you catch it there? Through the knowledge of HIM; that's how we get His power. Be in His Word. Listen to what He is sharing through His Word. Record it in your journal to refer back to on tough days and as you make decisions.

2. Trust Until His Promise Comes True: Prayer

Like Joshua heading into battles to overtake the Promised Land or David as he went out yet again to fight the Philistines during his kingship, they checked in with God every time.

Every time they were successful they sought God for the exact plan He had. He gave it to them everytime. He will do the same for us. They did not assume God would do it the same as He did it the time before. They were constantly asking Him for guidance and direction. He leads, guides and directs us into the exact purpose and vision He has for us and gives all the power needed to walk it out!

The only question is - will you let Him?

James 5:16(b) ESV shares:

> *"The prayer of a righteous person has great power…"*

That is absolutely true and was the key to sky-rocketing our ministry from nothing to impacting hundreds of lives deeply in just a few short years. The ways to pray and how to pray are endless. Specific, directed and corporate prayer are all things we do and spend lots of time teaching our clients how to do well.

3. Remembering Your Personal Journey with Him: Journaling

I cannot even begin to process and write of all He has done in my life! Most of that has been the result of slowing down and trusting in His power and not my own!

Ephesians 3:20 NLT sums it up best:

> *Now all glory to God, who is able, through His mighty power at work within us, to accomplish infinitely more than we might ask or think.*

How do we steward all that He shares? The better we steward, the more He will share.

Daily journaling of things like:

> Thank you Lord for...
> Confession of how you haven't been trusting in Him.
> What do you want me to focus on today?

Weekly journaling things like:

> Where is my identity?
> Who is He to me and my life?
> What lie am I believing?

When I'm scattered, angry, anxious or depressed, I know I am believing a lie and living a lie in some area of my life. These questions help me identify where that lie is hiding. As I ask these questions and answer them honestly, life gets easier and easier. I am relieved of the pressure of feeling like I need to control others or circumstances. I can walk my walk with Him with ease and grace.

CRAZY STEP: REST

You can gather 100X the fruitfulness with 10X less time and energy if you do what He is calling you instead of doing EVERYTHING. You will be able to do it with ease and grace! Look at the Bible study story I shared earlier in this chapter; it's now changing the entire community. I could share numerous other examples of the same thing.

A bigger part of our spiritual, emotional, mental, and physical journey is working from sabbath rest. The Bible is full of places where it talks about rest and the importance of rest. Daily personal and weekly times of quiet with God for personal ministry are necessary for success.

Silent retreats have been one of the absolute keys to getting a clear connection with God and experiencing His power. They clear away clutter and bring clarity like nothing else. Just God and the space and attention for Him to speak to you: no people talking, temptation to run to technology, nothing.

Have your journal handy as He will reveal so much.

In my silent retreats, God has revealed character traits that I need to allow Him to work me through. He has told me: well done, slow down, get moving, be careful, don't worry. He has also warned me about the upcoming calamities. He has even downloaded full events and books in my mind! He first started revealing many things through dreams and visions during my silent retreat time.

Our most successful fundraisers, including a recent one where we raised $30,000+ in just a few hours, God downloaded to me at a silent retreat. During my silent retreat, within a few minutes, He shared the name, theme, script for the evening and also the guest list. The Board and I spent the next few months walking that vision out with ease and grace. It was our best event ever, both in planning, execution and financial reward for the time invested. Many are even talking about coming from around the country next year! All because we took the time to listen and connect with His power and not our own.

Quiet time pulled away for Him; away from Netflix, social media, house cleaning, family responsibilities and other life distractions is a sacrifice and He rewards. Don't miss this powerful way to connect and get clarity directly from the source of the Maker of Heaven and Earth! He will speak to you, but you will need to stop and listen.

God has the power to walk this out, not you. Trusting God, when it doesn't look possible, is easier when we remember the Bible's history of Him, remember your history with Him, trust Him until the promise He made comes true and enjoying rest with Him in the meantime! Journaling in its many forms helps us to steward what He is telling us and remember it. Rest is critical to success.

How do we consistently rely on His power? We may need to take on a remodeling project of sorts, which is the focus of our next chapter together.

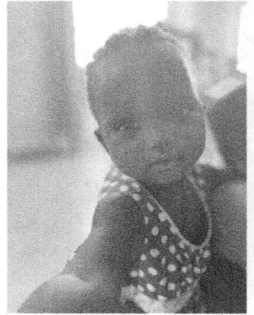

CHAPTER 3
FOUNDATION UNDER CONSTRUCTION: CHARACTER (SELF LEADERSHIP)

God's power is critical to moving your nonprofit forward. You need to let God into the foundation of your heart, mind, and emotions to be able to handle God's power in any significant measure. As much as emotions and burdens are critically important and good for vision and mission setting, emotions can also be toxic to your nonprofit ministry leadership success.

We will never be able to live out His purpose and power if we are constantly being tossed to and fro by our emotions and other people's actions and behaviors. Some common pitfalls are:

People-pleasing.
Comparing ourselves to others.
Wallowing in the deep pain of betrayals and unfair circumstances for long periods.
Lashing out in emotional outbursts at people around us.
Sticking our head in the sand; pretending things are not affecting us, but we stop trying, trusting and doing.

These will all keep you living in a sea of emotional ruin if you let it. They are all distractions and will keep us from moving forward strongly. Lack of emotional healing leads to disobedience and unhealthy ways of interacting with people.

Remember when you were a child and you skinned your knee? Remember the spray your mom would put on your knee before applying the band aid? It hurt so bad. I would avoid it at times. But avoiding it led to infection and lots of long term problems. Dealing with your emotions is the spray. It will prevent and pull out infection; leaving more space for Him and increase your effectiveness and quality of your leadership!

Jonah was a prophet the Lord used in the Old Testament. He is famous for his few overnights in the belly of a whale. As I was reading Jonah again recently it struck me how much Jonah's emotions overtook him and almost destroyed his life and testimony. The end of the book of Jonah scares me. I'm not sure where he stood with God when his time on this earth ended.

> *But God said to Jonah, "Is it right for you to be angry about the plant?" "It is," he said. "And I'm so angry I wish I were dead." Jonah 4:9*

I've been in the middle of my own emotional messes that I have let distract me too. I don't want you to be in the pit of emotional turmoil; so let's heal our emotions - have better leadership and end well with the Lord!

First, a word of caution, we all have emotional baggage to work through in our lives and God calls us to work through it. None of this is to condemn anyone.

> **This God is my strong refuge and has made my way blameless. 2 Samuel 22:33 ESV**

Keep this in mind as we read through Jonah's story and process through our own. Jesus' death on the cross took care of all of our sins and left us blameless. So let's clear the junk out of us so we can live the blameless life He died to give us!

RUNNING FROM GOD: DISOBEDIENCE HURTS OTHERS

In Jonah 1, we find him in deep-seated emotions of anger and fear. His hatred and terrifying fear were not unfounded. Nineveh was the capital of a longtime enemy of Israel and known for its great wealth, power, and prestige. Notorious for cruelty and idolatry (See Nahum 3:19). To Jonah, Nineveh and Israel was like God forgiving without visible punishment those that carried out the 9-11 attacks on the US. These emotions held him back from heading to the nation God was calling him to. Instead of dealing with his emotions, Jonah hopped on a ship to run from where God called him. By doing that he created a world of trouble in his life and the lives of those around him.

Our sin and rebellion affects other people both near and far. Jonah's running led to a shipwreck. (See Jonah 1:4-16) Jonah's sin caused suffering for other people; some that were near him - sailors. Others that were far and never even met him - the people that put cargo on the ship that never made it to the port. Our sin and rebellion affects other people too. Those we lead and serve- family, clients, staff, volunteers.

Let's deal with our emotions directly with God so others don't suffer.

EVEN IN THE MESS… GOD IS THERE

Jonah had consequences for himself. He was thrown overboard and lived in the belly of a whale - not the best accommodations - for a few days. (See Jonah 1:17)

Despite Jonah's disobedience, God provided protection. God provided a "room" in the belly of a whale for a few days. While in his "room", Jonah gave us a great example of what to do when we are going the wrong direction and emotions are overrunning us. He prayed. Jonah 2 is a powerful example of prayer for us:

Verse 3 - Crying out, being honest with how he felt when God hurled him into the depths of the waves and breakers. Crying out with our honest feelings brings peace.

Verses 6(b)-7(a) - But you, Lord my God, brought my life up from the pit. "When my life was ebbing away, I remembered you, LORD, and my prayer rose to you". This is key; do we remember Him and keep our focus on Him?

Verse 8 - Those who cling to worthless idols turn away from God's love for them. OUCH! In Jonah's case it was the idol of his emotions that he let distract him from what God was calling him to do.

What about you and me? In what ways are we turning to idols instead of God's love? Is it money, people, stuff, Netflix, social media, computer games? How often do we allow our emotions to distract us? Overcome us? Stop us from acting? Or spill over onto others around us? Do we take our emotions to God and look to His Word to define us or others around us?

Those are painful realizations for me to acknowledge. But once I do then I can receive all the grace, mercy, love, and anything else I need from Him.

Despite all of his running, God also displays his loving kindness and mercy to Jonah again and again as he cries out to Him. The same compassion and grace He showed Jonah, He also shows us. We just need to ask for it!

MISSION ACCOMPLISHED BUT ANGER RETURNS

In Chapter 3, Jonah, after pouring out his emotions out to God, now heads to Nineveh and delivers his quick message. (Jonah 3:4 Jonah ...... proclaiming, "Forty more days and Nineveh will be overthrown.")

Nineveh believes God and heeds the warning, fasts, sackcloths, seeks and calls urgently on God, giving up their evil ways and violence. (Jonah 3:3-10) It's believed over 100,000 people changed their ways that day! Lots to celebrate.

Despite this, Jonah let his anger at God for being a gracious and compassionate God, slow to anger and abounding in love overcome him. (Jonah 4:2(b)) This shows us that dealing with our emotions is not a one and done experience. It is a constant circling.

After such a powerful prayer experience in the whale's belly, you would think Jonah was all set for life, but that wasn't the case. He had more emotions that he needed to take to God for healing.

WHERE JONAH'S ANGER STEMMED FROM

If Jonah had taken his emotions to God he would see, he, just as much as those in Nineveh, was in need of God's grace, compassion, and love. Instead, he chose to focus on his emotional response to these people over what God was telling him and asking him to do. Jonah of course felt his judgment of these people was just and right.

He refused to realize that he needed that same grace, compassion and love and that he equally, didn't deserve it.

The same is true for us. The person that is driving us crazy with their behavior is a child of God. Just like Jonah, we need to change our heart and focus on taking our emotions to God so that we are better equipped to lead others and work with clients in our nonprofit work.

The story of Jonah shows us that, if God calls us, He will find us. He has total control over this world. For Jonah it was a storm on the sea. For us it might be allowing our emotions to overflow onto our kids, sickness, loss of a job, betrayal, overwhelming thoughts of starting a nonprofit.

I can relate to the story of Jonah because, just like him, I was trying to run away from my emotions.

MY STORY: HIDING THE PAIN FROM GOD

The devil tried to use horribly painful circumstances to destroy my life and I gave him a good feeding ground for it by hiding. The shame, the rejection, the fear, the hurt were overwhelming. A pit that if I allowed myself to fall into, I didn't think I could ever get out. I pretended as if it didn't happen or that it wasn't not affecting my life. Just didn't think about it and it won't bother me. Probably similar to Jonah.

However, the pain was controlling my life. Under the surface, it governed every decision I made and my reaction. My story was owning me and making decisions for me, subconsciously like Jonah. I had no idea it was happening. I thought I was leading a good life. I didn't see the pain and bitterness in me. By ignoring and pushing down my emotions, I was giving the devil fertile ground to plant his seeds of lies and deception.

If I was really honest, I lived in fear people would "find out" the story behind my pain; find out I was not good enough, smart enough or just enough. I felt like a fraud and an imposter, waiting to be found out at any moment.

I hopped on the achievement train to overcome my thoughts of inadequacies. I had to keep moving forward and achieving something at all times to stay ahead of the emotions. I worked harder and longer to go after the best career and income; perfectionism and overachievement everywhere.

In the meantime, at various points of my life, I hid from the pain by excessive shopping, food intake, drinking, social media scrolling, excessive focus on my children and their activities and TV watching. Can you relate?

THE OTHER SIDE

As I started to take my story to God, through being in His Word, and by journaling, praying and other things, I was able to share my emotions with others. I experienced love, joy and peace like I had never experienced before. It was totally freeing. Nothing was hidden. I was an open book and there was nothing for anyone to "find out" about me. Complete freedom. I was now owning my story and knew I was loved and accepted exactly the way I was, despite all the pain and messes that were done to me and that I had done. If people judged me - their reaction was not my problem. God guided my heart and mind. I could leave them to their ideas and opinions and stay focused on what God was asking of me.

Now through the nonprofit God has called me to, I'm allowing Him to use the pain of my story to save, transform and redeem the lives of girls and babies in Kenya through Mercy's Light Family.

If I would have let my leadership be bogged down in old emotional hurts, etc., you wouldn't be seeing this and I and those closest to me would be miserable. Healing emotional hurts is key, but how do we do it?

CLEANING OUT HEART MOTIVES

Emotional healing removes debris from our life to let more of Him in and more of Him and His Word be absorbed. Here are some ways to work out that healing.

1. Being In The Word Personally And In A Community Setting At Church And In Group Bible Study.

This is critically important to transforming us into all God created us to be, so make sure that is part of your healing process. At times, I was in 6-7 group studies, in some form, each week; some with homework; others without any; and some studying with my kids. All different types. I needed to get my thoughts and emotions in check. Whatever the pace you need, get into the Word in corporate settings and also privately with Him.

2. Weekly Emotional Check-ins With Yourself.

Are you like me and hide your emotions or try to pretend they aren't affecting you?

I was shocked to read in Matthew 5:4 NIV a few years ago:

Blessed are those who mourn, for they will be comforted.

Did you see it? If I want to be comforted, I need to be willing to mourn. I spent a lot of my life being strong; showing no emotion; not letting anyone know that they hurt me. This verse is telling me to live differently.

So now I do emotional check-ins weekly in my journal. I draw circles for each of the following questions:

What am I MAD about from last week?
What makes me SAD from last week?
What am I GLAD about from last week?
Are there any other emotions that are in me right now?

As things come up, I take the time to journal through them right then or at least sometime during that week. As I journal, I ask specific questions of God and wait for Him to reveal the answers and write them out as He does:

What should I learn from this circumstance?
Am I to do anything in response to this circumstance other than bring it to you?

If He leads, I will take any next steps. Most of the time, He is revealing things for me specifically and I rarely have to go back to other people. When I do, I ask Him how to best approach the conversation so I don't let my emotions get in the middle of it and make the circumstance worse. Because I check in often, I can have these conversations with ease and grace, and not get overwhelmed and anxious because my emotions are in check with Him.

3. Coach Or Community Once A Month For Check-Ins.

I started the weekly emotional check-ins at the direction and oversight of a coach. Knowing I was going to have to share with my coach in a few weeks kept me accountable.

In addition to accountability, which is huge, having someone you are checking in with regularly can help reveal things you might not be seeing. That person can help reveal things you might be blind to, both good and difficult things.

4. Going Deeper In Emotionally Stuck Areas.

If you have areas that are a constant source of emotional pain, maybe a circumstance or a relationship, or you're just starting your emotional healing journey, you're going to need more than this book. You might need a counselor like I did to help you process through some of the deep pain. Once you do the deep work, these exercises, and many resources we have at the back of this book and on our website, can help with maintenance.

However you do this work, just make sure you do it for yourself and all those around you. Even though trudging through our emotions is a difficult and sometimes tearfilled process, it is worth it! Emotional healing is a continual process between you and the Lord, but you will see some signs as you are fully owning your story. The results will show you why it's worth the journey. It brings complete freedom!

SIGNS YOU ARE HEALING EMOTIONALLY: WHY IT IS WORTH IT!

People that offend you don't bother you as much.
Not blaming, justifying, and excusing your actions, despite other people's actions. As we get emotional healing we take responsibility for ourselves and realize these things give our power over to others.

Not comparing yourself or your organization to what others are doing. You will be too busy focusing on Him.

Alerts will rise if the desire to people-please creeps into your life so you can fight against it. You will sense an unrest when you creep into relying on education, classes, achievement, or anything else instead of relying on Him for whatever He may be calling you to do. He may call you to some of these outlets, but then you will have peace.

You can allow others to make their choices and your emotions are not affected by them - even when you know they are making bad decisions. You can leave them to their choices and love them anyway, just like Jesus loves you when you make yours.

You are quick to forgive and slower to anger.

You are living out what the Word of God calls you to more than you are not. We are always a work in process. Our thoughts and actions should be more and more conformed to His image everyday.

In short, you will be working *from* His love, not *for* His love. This will make a difference in every area of your life!

We have been through the crawling stages of beginning of vision and mission! We have our own spiritual, mental and emotional healing started and a priority. It's finally time! Our nonprofit baby is about to begin WALKING! Let's read on to see what our first baby steps are.

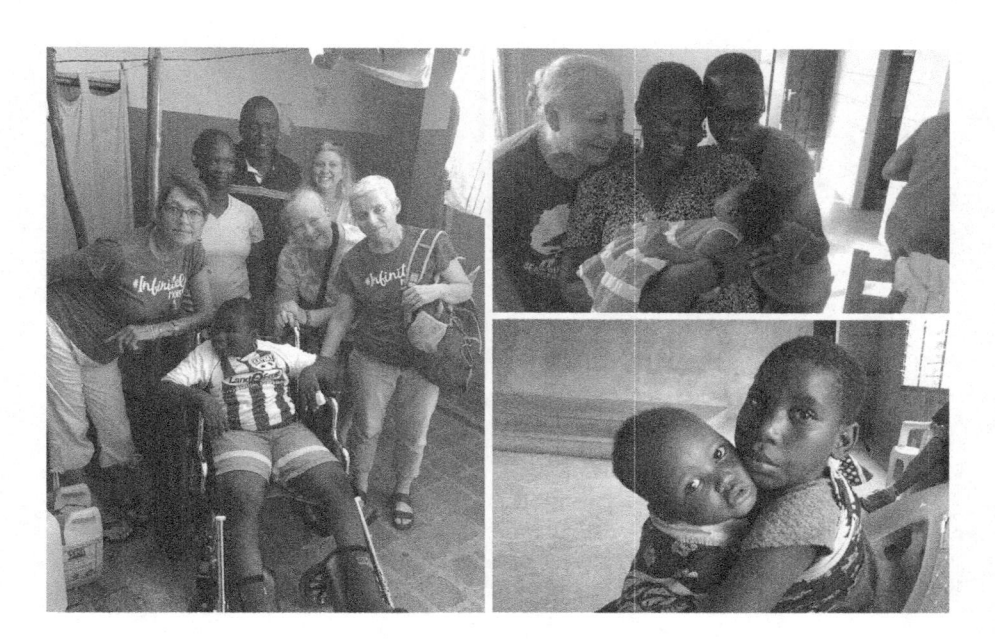

CHAPTER 4
START SMALL: KEEP GOING

Once our emotions are in check and being watched over in a safe place regularly, we are better leaders. Now it's time to take concrete steps in developing the mission. Be forewarned, these steps may not look like the final version of the vision and mission He has for you. First, you need to choose faith and not fear no matter what. Then you can start taking some action in baby steps and just keep going!

FAITH OVER FEAR

This world is a scary place. Physical, emotional, financial, political; pain and unrest. The TV news, computer home screens, and newspapers all surround us with it. We must choose faith over fear, but how?

There were times when I crawled forward because I was so afraid I couldn't walk. It's okay to feel afraid. That's normal. But don't let the fear stop you! Do it afraid!

Stand on God's Word. Like 2 Timothy 1:7 NIV:

> *For the Spirit God gave us does not make us timid, but gives us power, love and self-discipline.*

For me, it was becoming a published author. I hated English class and never wanted to be a writer. I was beyond terrified when I sent my first book to an editor let alone publish it and let the whole world read my journal and thoughts.

Another example is when I was heading out on a mission trip and I had a 103 degree fever (pre-CoVid days). The doctor gave me permission to travel but I seriously didn't know if I could do it. But after the 1.5 hour drive to the airport, the illness mysteriously lifted and I was fine.

Going to donors in person and online asking for donations and knowing some will reject me was also agonizing.

Public speaking and setting up events to share my vision and mission was also very hard for me. I hated public speaking and I didn't even know how to effectively share. How about when one person shows up to your event? Will you go all in for that one person?

These are the testing grounds; not of your abilities or bodily strength, but God is testing our hearts and our motives. Will we be faithful to Him and do it well for the one? Or do we need an audience of a certain number to go all in. Will we rely on Him? We get to choose faith or fear. Which will you choose?

Why do I share this? To give you examples that when you are walking out God's vision, it's His job to bring the **pro**vision, not yours! It's our job to choose faith! It's His job to produce results through our faithful steps of obedience. Now I see these same results in our clients at Christian Rocketeers as they push into Him!

WHAT STANDS IN THE WAY OF A FAITH OVER FEAR LIFE?

Pride is the biggest thing that stands in the way of a faith-filled life. Pride is putting yourself above God - an inordinate love of one's own excellence; your thoughts, your ideas, your education, your plans, your abilities, your ways, your money. Pride shows up the sneakiest of ways. We are all familiar with the: I'm better than everyone else scenario.

Pride is also in: I'm not good enough. I don't have enough. These statements imply and say that Jesus' death on the cross was not enough for you. I know we don't think about that when we say them but it's the truth. Joyce Meyer shared this with me years ago and it has stuck: we can choose pitiful or we can choose powerful, but we cannot choose both. Each moment we are making a choice.

Pride also shows up as perfectionism. It needs to be perfect. It needs to be perfect now, or I'm not coming back to this.

You may be a perfectionist if you:

- Have high standards and expectations - have difficulty overlooking small mistakes; rigid black-or-white thinking patterns; spend time judging others in accordance with your high standards
- Feel pressured to live up to high expectations
- Constantly planning/organizing and rarely actually doing; always needing exact rules, expectations, and instructions
- Exaggerated fear of failure; viewing any mistake as failure or incompetence
- Intense fear of being rejected or judged because of mistakes; hypersensitivity to criticism

As I studied this list I saw more of myself on this list than I want to admit. How about you?

If not, here are some real life examples of pride/perfectionism:

I don't want to start something smaller than the big vision God has shown me. I self fund only. God told me to solely fund. I don't need to ask for help. I don't need anyone's help.

Other people always disappoint me or don't follow through. I will just do it all myself.

I'm going to do what God tells me to do. I don't need any other authority, guides or mentors.

I'll copy what XYZ is doing without direction from God on what you should be doing.

The list could be endless; these are ones I see a lot. These thoughts are the devil keeping you stuck. Let's unlock some keys to overcoming.

KEYS TO WALKING OUT OF FEAR & PRIDE

God shared something with me as I was praying. The root of fear and pride is: not being willing to walk away from whatever is stealing your identity away from Me. That could be money, stuff, time, education, other people, my own abilities.

Here are some ways to overcome fear and pride:

1. Identify Where We Are Pulling Our Identity From

If my identity is in Christ, what happens in this world doesn't need to affect me at a deeper level.

For example, I am walking in obedience to what God is calling me to do, I don't need to worry about it. It is God's problem to solve, not mine. He doesn't need my abilities to do it. If I am pulling my identity from my abilities, I would have a lot to worry about. All the things I mentioned above and more!

Where are we pulling our identity from? God's Word and what He says? What I think or feel? What others think and feel?

Our mindsets are cultivated from what we are filling our time and life with.

2. What Am I Filling Up On

If I want more faith and to pull my identity from Him, I need to make choices to fill myself with things that bring my faith and Him to the forefront and put away things that bring out fear and self reliance.

See if God speaks to you from this list or spurs another area for you:

Turn off the news. Turn on the audio Bible or a sermon.
Change your computer home screen to a promise in the Word you need to be reminded of right now not current events.
Hang out with people doing things He is calling you to.
Take different risks.
Spend less time on social media scrolling and more time in the Bible app, prayer, Bible study.
TV. (I tell myself it's my resting time, but really I'm not resting. I'm filling myself with something. It might not be sinful but it still might not be life giving.) Stream a sermon or a movie filled with Him.

Are you willing to make the changes to have a "FAITH over fear" life and put pride away? If you want different results, you have to be willing to do different things. It only takes a few minutes a day filling ourselves with more of Him and the whole world looks very different tomorrow!

3. Rest In His Promises Not My Abilities

To live the faith over fear life we have to have confidence in His faithfulness not ours. We must stop looking at the current circumstances around us to determine whether God is actually going to do what He says He is going to do. Trust Him and take Him at His Word.

To do that we need to be in the Word. Beth Moore, in her study *Believing God*, had us repeat some powerful statements that have stuck with me. I may be paraphrasing them but here is what we need to know and remember:

God is who He says He is.
God can do what He says He can do.
I am who He says I am.
His Word is Alive and Active in this world today!

All of these things are found in His Word. He makes good on His promises! If He is leading you, He will handle the details. Let Him lead. Our ministry is living proof of that. Our clients ministries' are living proof of that. Your body working, this world being held together and so many more examples could be shared.

I love Joshua 21:45 which says:

> *Not one of all the Lord's good promises to Israel failed; everyone was fulfilled.*

Standing on His promises was the critical turning point for me and it will be for you. Don't stand on you and the circumstances around you.

4. Let Go Of Control And Step Into His Authority & Community

When I started this journey I felt I needed more control. If I had more control this would work out better and faster. Now I know I don't need control, I need authority. Good news!

Luke 9:1 NKJV shares:

> *Then he called his twelve disciples together, and gave them power and authority over all devils, and to cure diseases.*

Matthew 28:18 NKJV shares:

Then Jesus came to them and said, **"All authority in heaven and on earth has been given to me.**

If He has called you, He has given you all you need to do this nonprofit! You need to submit to HIS authority and stop trying to work in your own control.

What has He called you to exercise power and authority over in the world? That's all we need to be clear on. That's what we work hard with our clients to get clarity around. Then, as we stay inside our area of power and authority from Him we will see miracle after miracle!

5. Community and Corporation Prayer

Living in community with others doing similar work is critical for keeping us from going astray and into pride or staying stuck in fear. Coaching. Corporate Bible studies. Close partners can all help here.

Also, you need to have at least three people that are super close to the ministry that you are praying with and making decisions with. We will talk more about that in the people chapters. I trust certain donors, friends well grounded in the Word, and workmates that I make decisions with. I never make a large decision alone.

It is key to have time in the Word together and times of corporate prayer together. Come together and bring your problems before God together as a group and ask for wisdom and guidance. You will be amazed at the things God will bring to mind when you come together in prayer. This can be by phone, or in person. We do this often, even before we have problems.

IT'S TIME TO TAKE ACTION

God honors baby steps, He doesn't honor attempts at perfection. He is the only one who is perfect and is the only one that needs to be! You just do what He is calling you to!

Get SOMETHING done. Don't wait for everything to be perfect. Just get moving, He will work with that. To be able to live in God's power, we must take action, His Word requires it! (James 2:26)

> *For the kingdom of God does not consist in talk but in power....*
> I Corinthians 4:20 ESV

> *Do not merely listen to the word, and so deceive yourselves. Do what it says.*
> James 1:22 NIV

At the beginning, your action is unrelated to ministry. It is everything to get your life consistent to His Word so you are ready for Him to flow through you like a pipeline!

1. It Starts With Love

How we LOVE matters, even in difficult circumstances and with difficult people. Be loving to everyone in your home and family; especially the person that rubs you the wrong way. Then be loving to the clerks in the grocery store - even when you're super busy and the line is long! Constantly look for ways to spread His love to everyone around in small ways. Especially when the person doesn't deserve it.

Examples of this could fill a whole book and are deeply personal, but I'll share one.

One May morning in my quiet time, I was bringing a circumstance with extended family before Him, asking for answers of why they couldn't be nicer and why we needed to deal with this behavior, and He said "Carrie, I want you to go and buy them an inflatable baby pool and fill it with summer fun things for their little baby and leave it on their porch."

I was like, aren't you hearing me?
I want healing.
I want you to make them apologize.
I want this made right.

He said "I am. Just do it."

So I headed to Walmart and bought the items. I inflated the pool in the car and placed the other things inside. I then checked to see if the coast was clear and ran it up to their porch and left it unsigned and unnoticed.

I began the process with a "what about me" tone, but, once it was over, my hurt fell away and was replaced with love and real prayers FOR them. My love came from Him, I didn't need theirs. They could be who they were and I didn't need my emotions or attention to be focused on them. I was focused on Him instead.

Your circumstance could be very different and He will lead you. Be willing to bring it to Him and do what He says, even if you don't want to. Keep your eyes focused on Him.

How do you do this? It is only possible if we allow Him to love on us every morning in our one-on-one time with Him in all the ways we have outlined. He will reveal it for you!

2. It Moves To Forgiveness

I have had to forgive some major things - rape and sexual abuse, divroce, affairs, betrayals, etc. So let me start by saying "I get it." It's hard and not fair. They don't deserve it.

Forgiveness *only* goes to those that don't deserve it. And God reminds us that we receive forgiveness from Him when we didn't deserve it also.

He also goes on to show us in life and in His Word, unforgiveness is actually not hurting the other person. It's keeping us in a prison of hurt and anger; a prison that we hold the key to through forgiveness.

Forgiveness is not easy but it is freedom; freedom to let go of pain and hurt that we have caused or that others have caused. It is up to God to judge rightly and take vengeance as is appropriate. Forgiveness is worth it! It is part of the process for His power!

And it carries on with many other character traits from there in accordance with His Word! In the meantime it's time to get started!

CRAZY MISSION BABY STEPS

As we start to focus specifically on our vision and mission, God will lead us to do some crazy silly things especially as we get started. Because He wants us to remember and recognize this vision and mission is only working because of Him and not us. So if God directs it, you need to do it even when it seems crazy.

I'll never forget when fundraising for a project, before He released the vision of Mercy's Light, we were looking for a building. The price for a half done building came back at $50-80,000, depending on which property we chose. I was freaking out. There was only one thing I was sure of and that was I would NEVER be able to raise that amount of money! EVER!

I was alone in Kenya at the time and I dragged my extremely anxious head to the beach. Reminding God He had called a lawyer; not a fundraiser. I don't know how to ask for money or where to find it.

As I was repeating this over and over to Him in my head, the sound of the ocean caught my ear and then my sight. Then an inaudible whisper came to mind: "If I can hold this ocean in its shores with its rhythmic waves day and night for however long this earth has been in existence, don't you think I can raise $50-80,000?"

My mind said: "Yes. But *I don't know how to*."

Back in the house, I pulled out my laptop to write a blog post. As I did the cord got stuck in some bags. Struggling to break the cord free I heard another inaudible whisper: "Sell crafts."

"Sell crafts." That's crazy. That will never work. Have you been to a craft fair? They sell stuff for $1-5. We need $50,000. You must be joking.

But, as we did the crazy, He added other things to our plate and in just a short amount of time we had raised over $560,000 with very little effort and maintaining a healthy family life and lots of travel, including Kenya.

The moral of the story - just do it - even if it seems crazy.

Take daily baby steps toward His vision and purpose for you and you will see miracle after miracle! Just take baby steps along the way. What is He putting in front of you? Take those opportunities even if they seem crazy.

KEEP GOING

Shortly after Mercy's Light Family opened its doors to girls for the first time, a fellow board member that had seen the hardest parts of the journey from the inside asked "If you meet someone just starting the journey you went on, what one piece of advice would you give that person?" Immediately, without hesitation, the words "just keep going" came out of my mouth.

Even when it looks as though physically EVERYTHING has fallen apart, JUST KEEP GOING.
Even when nothing seems to be happening, JUST KEEP GOING.
Even when no one is there to help, JUST KEEP GOING.

Even when betrayal hurts so bad you don't think you will make it through, JUST KEEP GOING.
Even when you have no money, JUST KEEP GOING.
Even if all you know to do is go to Him in prayer and be in the Word, JUST KEEP GOING.

If it's a vision from God, it WILL come to pass. You just need to keep going! Do the small things and keep going. God will work out the details.

Keep close to God in relationship and make sure all you are doing is flowing from Him and not you. Spend time daily in the Word and prayer. Ask Him the next steps and do what He says! Some of the steps will seem crazy. Some may seem counterproductive. Trust Him! Start small but KEEP GOING.

You will have ups and downs in this process. Let's learn how to embrace those and sky-rocket to success!

CHAPTER 5
THERE'S PURPOSE IN THE PROCESS: EMBRACING & RELEASING

2015 was a very difficult year for me. Financially, I was losing my daycare business to the fear of an Ebola outbreak in Kenya. Though I know it was God's larger plan to move me from full time work to standing in the gap for voiceless girls of Kenya, it was extremely scary and painful. I loved the babies in my care and counted on the weekly income.

I was also in a dispute with the board of the first nonprofit I founded as to how I would raise mission support, which led me, after a year of waiting, to start another nonprofit.

As we were resolving that, a larger issue within the board arose. Someone shared they felt the mission God was calling me to in Kenya was not covered by our current mission statement.

Lacking personal funding, I only made it to Kenya for a short one week trip and I didn't have a vehicle so I spent most of the time in the house. I thought it was my farewell trip.

Add to that a speeding ticket, three speaking engagements I did with kidney stones, a child getting into a car accident, and a child coming to terms with a drug addiction and heading into treatment one week after I had to kick them out of our house.

It got so bad by August, I recall moments where I said, "If this is what following God looks like…I'm not sure I want it."

Though I didn't understand these circumstances or appreciate them in the moment, these painful moments set me up for amazing results soon after:

*Our first TV appearance was in September of the same year.
*That TV appearance has brought us credibility, recognition and results.
*Major partnerships - fundraising opportunities followed.
*A revamped and stronger board.
*Expansion of work beyond Kenya into the US and other parts of the world.
*Learned how to keep nonprofit board relationships and friendships separate.
*Learned how to handle opposition

God wanted to make sure I was not depending on anything but Him. This journey was all about teaching me I needed to be okay about letting go of things.

Letting go of expectations.
Letting go of a prior God given purpose (daycare).
Letting go of how I think things should be done.
Letting go of people - letting them have their own thoughts and opinions and being okay with that even if I don't agree.
Letting go of projects.
Letting go of everything but Him!

You will have these same moments in your nonprofit journey. Don't be surprised or alarmed. Don't think: "I'm doing this all wrong". In fact, it's the exact opposite. If these things are happening it's because you are on the right track. It's just the process. God's word warns us about it. (John 16:33) Take it like Paul and the disciples did - like a badge of courage!

Carrie Reichartz

THE SHAKE UP…EMBRACE REJECTION

My main concern was where would my income come from after the close of my business. This shake up led me into writing full-time with the goal of creating an income.

As I wrote articles and submitted them to various places, I started to receive rejection letters and it put my writing on hold. I didn't like getting rejected. The letters hurt and didn't feel good. All the work of putting my heart and soul out there only to be rejected. Not to mention all the time, energy and attention I was giving it. For what? A rejection letter? I needed finances to support myself and my family and this wasn't working.

As I took the hurt to God in prayer I heard an inaudible whisper…. EMBRACE REJECTION. Shoot for 100 rejection letters!

Once again, I wasn't happy with God's whisper. It made no sense. How is this solving the problem of feeding myself and my kids? But, as I embraced rejection, I was getting closer to my goal. If I got an article accepted it was a win! If I got a rejection letter I was one step closer to the needed 100! Not one day have I or my children gone without food, shelter, clothing, and many other wants.

Through this lesson God was teaching me. Rejection is not a reflection of who I am as a person. It is a reflection of timing, abilities (to pay and to write) and current needs. I am a child of God with or without acceptance of a writing submission or anything else.

Though I never did reach the 100 rejection letter goal, this lesson of embracing rejection has helped me in so many ways.

Later, I took these lessons into my fundraising efforts as well. If I'm not getting no's, then I'm probably not asking enough or for enough!

RELEASING AND EMBRACING

Rejection brought me to a whole new level of what I should be releasing and embracing in my life. The list could be endless so let me share a few.

RELEASE	EMBRACE
Failure	My response to take it to Jesus
Isolation	Community (even when I don't feel like it); Christ walked with the disciples even though they were not an easy bunch
Judging: self or others	Mercy and forgiveness
Trying to save people	Lead them to the One who can save them
Acceptance by family/people; Always being liked	Doing what God says; even if everyone doesn't agree; Pleasing God - not people
Comparison	Improving from YOUR yesterday not others; comparing yourself to Jesus not others
To-do list 1,000 miles long	Prayer with Him and doing what He says; usually 1-2 things per day
Control/Achievement	Surrendering to Him
Logic/ My thoughts: pride	His Word/His thoughts: humility
Quick results	The wait; knowing He is working; be active in prayer and obedience
Perfectionism (pride)	Getting started and grow
Hurts	Healing from God/forgiveness

People/Volunteers: promises	People's hearts; if they aren't getting work done, let them go but with love knowing their hearts were in the right place
Need for perfect circumstances	He has it all worked out
Old identity: shame, guilt, my abilities	I am a Child of God; freedom
Worldly reputation: what people say about you: titles	Complete and total acceptance from God no matter what you have done or left undone
Doing it alone: pride	Asking for help; community: humility
Worldly entertainment	Time with God
Complaining/Gossiping	Chatting with God and 2-3 inner circle people that lead you back to God
I'm not enough: pride	Jesus: He died to make you enough and God created you to be enough
Education	His leading and guidance - this may include some additional education but not doing education to gain feeling of confidence

This list is a powerful tool. I wish I had it when I started this journey. I wish I had time and space to share all the stories that go behind each and every item. They were lessons learned the hard way. You have them here without the pain, shame, guilt, waste of time and money that came from them. I hope you will take this blessing and make it a regular practice to revisit this list.

What do you need to release and embrace today to make you a better nonprofit leader and person?

WATCHING OUR THOUGHTS

I saw this quote from Toby Mac: Train your mind to hear what God is whispering to you, not what the enemy is shouting at you.

I think this is a great representation of what God's word says about our thoughts. Romans 12:1-2 (NIV) is my go to verse:

> .....in view of God's mercy, to offer your bodies as a living sacrifice, holy and pleasing to God—this is your true and proper worship. 2 Do not conform to the pattern of this world, but be transformed by the renewing of your mind. Then you will be able to test and approve what God's will is—his good, pleasing and perfect will.

Verse 1 tells us where to keep our focus - on all God has done for us.
Verse 2 tells us how and why to do that… renewing our mind so we can test and approve God's will.

How do we renew our mind?

HOW DO WE RENEW OUR MIND?

Being in the Word, prayer, corporate accountability groups, and being willing to do what God is calling you to do. Releasing and embracing is a huge part of that.

1. Writing and Asking Detailed Questions.

My husband and I recently felt God was leading us to move. He kept telling me "downsize", but we didn't know where He was leading us. While I looked at homes in Kenya, my husband looked at homes in Florida near the beach!

We committed to spending just 15 minutes a week asking specific questions of God and journaling and then we would share with each other what God revealed as we journaled.

Finally it dawned on us: should we release this decision to God and ask Him where He wanted us? We had some great ideas and wants; but when we got out our journals and asked "where do you want us to move?", within two minutes of journaling He revealed Atlanta.

We didn't jump then - we continued with the last thing He told us to do. Downsize. We watched for Him to confirm. Shortly after this journaling time, a friend at church, who had no idea we were even downsizing, prayed for me and said "I don't get this, but I keep seeing a peach pit and Georgia but I don't know what it means." I said "I do".

We then had another similar confirmation as God led us to a free place to stay as we figured out what God had for us in Atlanta.

Let me offer this warning: many people think any amazing opportunity has to be from God. That is not true. You need to hear from Him that it's the right opportunity for right now. That takes focused time and attention in prayer, both privately and corporately. It doesn't mean a ton of time, but it means time spent seeking Him and His mind on the matter and making sure it's not your mind or the devil's distraction.

2. Creative Journaling Or Other Time.

Spending time doing creative things helps us use the other side of our brain. When we do, we let go of control and logic and God can come in.

I am not an artist. I prefer words, but I can color with the best of them! I enjoy coloring Bibles and coloring books centered around Bible verses.

Sometimes I grab Bibles at Goodwill and use those to cut scripture out and diagram them into a Creative Journaling notebook I have.

Maybe for you it will be painting or dancing or some other form of creative expression. The different ways to use creative journaling are endless. Explore options that are of interest to you. Whatever it is, just walk it out with Him. Make sure you are recording what God is sharing with you, so you can refer back to it. You will see it is incredibly powerful.

This creative outlet:

Grounds me when I'm overwhelmed, gives me answers I've been waiting for a long time, and helps release my desire to control and or stress over issues.

As we keep our channels clear by keeping our mind, thoughts, words and actions in line with God's will and repenting and acknowledging when we don't; God will be with you, He will complete it; He promises to! (Isaiah 46:11, 1 Kings 8:56, Phil 1:6) These exercises and all the rest in this book help you to stay there!

3. **Gratitude Tracking.**

One of the most powerful things God had me do in this journey was to purchase a calendar that I kept near my bed. Every night I had to write three things I was grateful for that day.

It is a simple thing, but it has taught me a lot about myself and what is most important in my life. I always thought of myself as a project focused person because I am. I want to check things off the list so bad every day! However, my projects rarely got onto the gratitude list. Maybe 2 projects made the list the whole year, but people were always on the list instead. It changed my heart and my focus. It made me ready to be an effective leader by focusing on people not projects.

My gratitude journal helped me renew my mind on days when things overall went poorly and I was feeling down. Sometimes I had to dig deep to find something to be grateful for, but, once I reviewed the prior week's entries, my mind was back where it belonged… focused on Him and His goodness in my life.

How do we now push through when things are super tough. In those darkest hours? Let's walk through that together in our next chapter!

CHAPTER 6
WHERE ARE THE BATTLEFIELDS: WILL YOU KEEP GOING?

I could write a whole book on the ups and downs of ministry. There are impossible circumstances, hurtful people both inside and outside the organization, problems with negative self-talk, shame, guilt, grumbling and complaining. Just to name a few.

There is one person in the Bible that was no stranger to opposition and resistance. I think we can glean some helpful reminders by studying the book of Nehemiah. I heard a sermon on Nehemiah by Darius Daniels in late 2016 on building walls that changed my world. I thought I was nowhere near building a physical wall. At that time, the Mercy's Light project had been stalled for three years. Nothing was happening. It has been a year since I walked away from my income source with nothing happening at all on the Kenyan side. I also had 1-2 fundraisers a year on the US side while everything else seemed to go dormant. That was excruciating.

Studying Nehemiah over the years has taught me invaluable lessons about overcoming, and where to expect battles to come from when doing God's work. He has taught me how to keep going when times are tough, and he has taught me I will be fighting battles on three fronts: in my mind, outside the organization, and inside the organization.

INTERNAL MIND BATTLES

As a human being who was cupbearer to the king, Nehemiah didn't have what it took to do what God was calling him to. He was called to rebuild the walls of Jerusalem. Nehemiah didn't know the culture of Jerusalem. He had never been there. He didn't have the expertise in leadership to lead. He didn't have experience in building projects of any kind, especially ones in a foreign country. I'm sure his mind was trying to get him to believe he didn't have what it took to take on the mission God was calling him to.

I can relate to that struggle. I added extra years into my journey because I listened to that negative voice for way too long. How about you? Do any of these questions or statements resonate with you?

Can I handle all the logistics of a nonprofit?
Where would the funding come from?
I don't know how to fundraise.
Where do I even start? I don't know how to organize this.
I'm not smart enough, rich enough, or connected enough to embark on this nonprofit journey.

Whatever our own mind is telling you, you need to choose to seek and focus on the mind of Christ, not all the thoughts that pull us away from Him and His will for your lives. Being in the Word, church, group Bible study, having regular silent retreat times, being humble, honest and transparent with those around you to get and keep the mind of Christ will help keep you in the right mindset.

EXTERNAL MIND BATTLES

Nehemiah faced battles from people outside the organization. Sanballat and his friends were government officials outside of Jerusalem and they did everything they could to instill fear and distract Nehemiah from the work he was sent to do.

I remember many external forces coming against the work in my own journey. Almost all the donor sources in my network indicated *"we only donate locally"*, leaving me with very little funding sourcing from within my close network.

In Kenya, government employees often refused to help. I remember one meeting in downtown Mombasa, when we were looking for the rules and regulations of what a building would need for our maternity home. The government employee was sitting solo in an office full of cubicles. She pulled a sheet of paper from her drawer with the exact details we needed and had spent days trying to find it at various different government offices.

I asked her if we could get a copy of it and she said no. As she was chatting with others in my group in Swahili, I was hand copying the details on a piece of my own paper. When she saw me doing that, she put the piece of paper back in her top desk drawer and closed it up tight. She wanted a bribe from us and then she would have let us have the paper.

I left that office IRATE! There I was, spending thousands of dollars of my personal money getting back and forth to Kenya, trying to build something to support Kenyan girls and babies and this is the "help" I get? I just wanted to write down what we needed to comply with and they wouldn't allow me to do that!

Circumstances like these are meant to scare and distract you from the goal. Granted, sometimes they do a good job of it; but, if you want to be successful in this journey and quickly succeed, you are going to have to get over the anger because staying focused on grumbling and complaining will never help you move forward.

Here are a few verses that helped me in that letting go process, maybe they will help you too:

> *... there is no authority except from God, and those that exist have been instituted by God.* Romans 13:1(b) ESV

..."O Lord, God of our fathers, are you not God in heaven? You rule over all the kingdoms of the nations. In your hand are power and might, so that none is able to withstand you. 2 Chronicles 20:6 ESV

...O Lord, glorious in power, your right hand, O Lord, shatters the enemy. Exodus 15:6 ESV

I press on toward the goal to win the prize for which God has called me heavenward in Christ Jesus. Philippians 3:14 NIV

GRUMBLING/COMPLAINING WILL NEVER GET YOU THERE

I remember a specific trip where many ministries were having trouble with an employee. There was so much frustration. It was a constant topic of conversation and the problems were affecting so much of the work. We were all suffering because of it. It was tempting, very easy and even inviting to constantly complain about this person. Complaining about anyone or anything will never get you to the next level. Just like the Isrealites in the wilderness, He doesn't take well to grumbling and complaining. (Exodus 16:12)

One of the most painful ministry breakups happened for many reasons. This was a breakup so big that I wasn't sure parts of our ministry would continue. This person was one of my right hand people for many years. As I was sitting on the couch in tears for weeks, God revealed many reasons for this break up. Most not specific to me, but one that was specific to me involved grumbling and complaining. On my end, it ended because God was calling me to stop reaching out to this person to "vent" (grumbling and complaining). And I wasn't doing that. He finally had to remove the option of doing that!

Nehemiah stayed focused on prayer and God, and not the problem of the people or his circumstances. Do the same because that will be what leads you to victory. That doesn't mean ignoring problems, it means take them to Him for answers.

This is God's project and He will work out the details in His perfect timing. If it isn't coming together yet, it's because it's not His timing yet. Your job is to stay focused on the prize - Christ and living a life consistent with Him with His help - and let God take care of those standing in your way of doing His will.

BATTLES INSIDE THE ORGANIZATION - STRIFE

By far the most hurtful and difficult battles are ones that involve internal strife. Specifically, the strife received from people within the project. For Nehimiah, the Jewish people were turning on themselves - charging ridiculous amounts of interest and not supporting each other. In my work it is usually the board, staff, or volunteers.

When we started this nonprofit and now as we start specific projects, I needed to raise money. One way I decided to do that was through social media and email campaigns outlining the needs by sharing stories I had been exposed to while in Kenya.

As I did, I received a message from a Kenyan that was deep in the mission with me. I was shocked. She condemned me and my knowledge of the reality of Kenya to pieces. It tore me up. On the US side, I'm getting message after message: "We only donate locally. You should be working locally". Now my lead Kenyan person at the time was messaging me that I have no idea what I'm talking about as I outline the needs that I have seen with my own eyes first hand.

That stung. I quit for the day, but the next day I was right back at the fundraising and getting the message out. My solution? I took it to God in prayer. I reached out for prayer from others. I asked two people that knew both of us to review the message and give me feedback. After doing those things, I realized her lashing out was between her and battles she was fighting within herself and had nothing to do with me and what God was calling me to do or how He was calling me to do it.

The secret to bouncing back involves one of the keys we covered earlier in this book, passion. Knowing that He has called you through your own personal story (and a lot of times pain) gives you the passion to keep pushing through. It keeps you focused on the purpose even when times are hard and people are coming against you. Passion fuels our purpose even in the midst of internal and external battles.

I'll never forget the pain of when a board member, someone I considered a close friend, came strongly against me. I was in a huge transition time. Ebola was in the midst of closing my only income source - a home day care. It was a devastating time in my heart. I was scared to walk away from income into nothing. My heart was breaking saying goodbye to babies I had in my care since they were 3 months old that were now turning 4 years old.

I sent a very casual, friendly email throwing out some ideas and asking some of the board to help me brainstorm ways for me to raise personal support, but also ensure I wouldn't pull from funds that I didn't personally raise so none of the program funds would be touched.

The response I received back shocked me. I received a LENGTHY email outlining how what I was asking for was illegal and they didn't feel my project even belonged under the OGH umbrella. Not a phone call. Just a super long email attacking me personally and the work as a whole. So now not only was the support an issue but they were trying to kick my whole program out. Out of a nonprofit that I did all the work to start both on the US and Kenyan side.

This shocking email came from someone I never would have expected. She is one of the nicest people I ever met after taking it to God to heal my heart, we are still friends today.

The devil will use people both outside and inside your organization and your own head to sabotage God's work. Like 1 Peter 5:8 NIV warns:

> *Be alert and of sober mind. Your enemy the devil prowls around like a roaring lion looking for someone to devour.*

The key to overcoming these oppositions is to realize they are normal. They happen all the time. They happened way back in Nehemiah's day, they happened to Jesus, they happened to Paul and they happen ALL the time today. Don't be shocked. Don't be worried. That is not to say they don't hurt. These hurt the WORST! These hurts come from places you never expected them to and come up out of the blue over something seemingly so small.

WHO REALLY WINS?

The examples of the opposition I've faced are endless. When first starting out, there was much more we faced. Now, it happens very rarely. So hang in there and don't give up because we know who wins.

The victory is ours if we are following what Christ is calling us to do.

Use these moments of opposition as a sign that you are on the right path. If the devil is not coming against your work, you're on the wrong path. He's not paying attention because you are already distracted and on the wrong path.

It happens to everyone on the path of following their passion. Abe Lincoln had a strong passion for building a great country. Do you think he let a few failures stop him from that? He ran in many elections that he did not win. When he finally was elected, life was not easy (civil war), but look at his place in history now.

Did you know the founder of Starbucks was turned down for a loan 275X at the start of his journey? Did that stop him? If it did you might not have had your coffee in the same way this morning.

JUST KEEP GOING

Don't give up. God will make a way where there doesn't seem to be one. As you lean into Him, He will work out the details. He will bring the victory, not you. The victory will be even sweeter after the battles you overcome through Him! JUST KEEP GOING!

Of course you are probably thinking, "That's nice Carrie, but how do I carry on when I just don't have anything left?" Don't worry my friend, we cover that in great detail in our Christian Rocketeers courses and coaching. I will cover some main points in the next chapter.

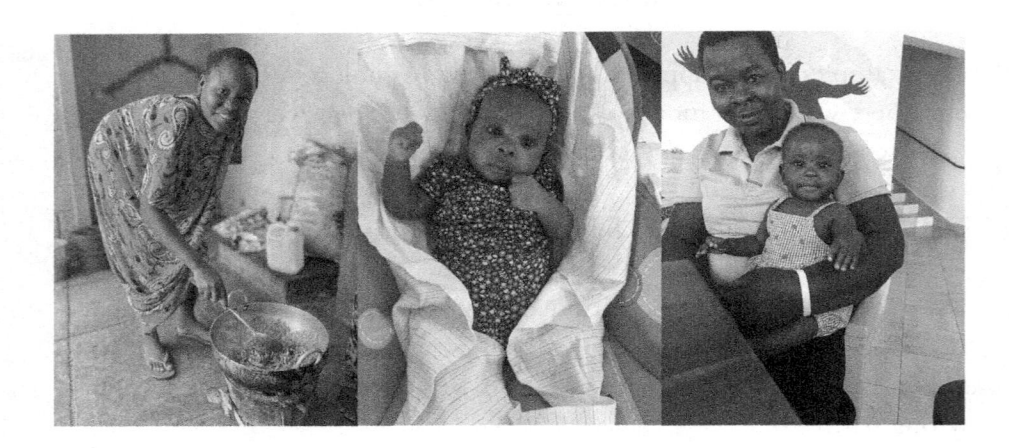

CHAPTER 7
FIGHTING BACK

Christian leadership involves opposition. Critics increase as we step into all that God has created us for. The greater the responsibility we are given, the greater the resistance we will face. The Bible is clear about that: Jesus and the Pharisees, you and your board, family and others.

While we can't control the opposition we face, we can control how we respond to it. Will you see it as a sign you are going the right direction? Or will you use it as an excuse to give up?

What do you do when the battle is unfair and about to break you financially, emotionally, or spiritually?

How you respond to opposition matters. It reveals your deep character. Is it your image or your integrity that's most important to you? Opposition reveals all of these characteristics. If you act with integrity, you will do and say the right thing regardless of what others do.

Romans 16:25 ESV gives us guidance on how to do that. It shares:

> *Now to **him who is able to strengthen** you according to my gospel and the preaching of Jesus Christ, according to the revelation of the mystery that was kept secret for long ages*

He is able to strengthen us. That is true. His Word says it. But how?

I've been through many battles over the years. Some battles I didn't think I would survive. Some I didn't think the organization would survive. Christian Rocketeers was birthed so no one else would have to endure those battles alone. It was born to equip Christian nonprofit leaders ahead of time to avoid or be ready for battles that come. Having a Christian-based cheerleader and encourager to link arms with on the journey, reminding you of the exact vision God shared with you and equipping you to get back to that vision together, is essential to your success.

There are many ways to prevent and help us through those battles. Here we will focus on four tactics: preventing attacks, watching our words, declaring the vision and keeping it before us, and how to handle a breach of security!

PREVENTING ATTACKS

The best defense is a good offense. Being in the Word and praying daily is the best offense. In Ephesians 6:10-18, Paul shares with us how to put on the **Whole Armor of God** as our defense! Let's pull it apart a bit.

10 *Finally, be strong in the Lord and in the strength of his might.*

Where does our strength come from? If it is ourselves we will constantly fail. It is in Him, even when circumstances don't look right, even when I don't feel right. His strength remains. He is holding up your budget, program, family, life, not you.

11 *Put on the whole armor of God, that you may be able to stand against the schemes of the devil.* **12** *For we do not wrestle against flesh and blood, but against the rulers, against the authorities, against the cosmic powers over this present darkness, against the spiritual forces of evil in the heavenly places.*

Imagine you showed up to play a football game, but you were playing on a baseball diamond. No matter what you do, it's not going to matter. You're not in the right field. You don't have the right equipment, focus or goals to play football on a baseball diamond.

Remembering that our battles are fought on the spiritual battlefield, not the world's, helps us keep perspective. Make sure to fight your battles in the right field.

13 *Therefore take up the whole armor of God, that you may be able to withstand in the evil day, and having done all, to stand firm.*

STAND….. Just stand. That's all you need to do. God will fight the battle for you. Stand on the Word of God and prayer.

14 *Stand therefore, having fastened on the belt of truth, and having put on the breastplate of righteousness,*

Again… STAND…. Because you put on His truth and righteousness; not standing on what the world says is the best next step; not standing on having all the funds in the bank; not standing on anything but His truth (found in the Word) and His righteousness (not our perfect behavior or actions). STAND.

15 *and, as shoes for your feet, having put on the readiness given by the gospel of peace.*

God gives us His peace as a fruit of the spirit. Practice it when emotions rise up in you. When others hurt you or confuse you, take it to Him, don't spew it out on other people. Bring peace to others and take your hurt to Him. Be ready by taking time to pull out old emotional stings and working them through with Him.

16 *In all circumstances take up the shield of faith, with which you can extinguish all the flaming darts of the evil one;*

In what circumstances? The easy ones? The non important ones? No, in ALL circumstances take up faith. Faith is: trusting what He says in His Word to be truth and standing on it no matter what the world around you looks like. Doing that extinguishes the devil's flaming darts, whatever they are!

17 *and take the helmet of salvation, and the sword of the Spirit, which is the word of God,*

Salvation is a critical piece to this as His power and strength are only available to those who take refuge in His salvation. Colossians 2:12 tells us:

> *having been buried with him in baptism, in which you were also raised with him through faith in the* ***powerful working of God, who raised him from the dead.***

Do you want the power that raised Christ from the dead working for you? Good news - if you have accepted Christ as your savior, you have that available! It's just a matter of taking the time to focus on it and act according to His will.

Then the only offensive weapon we need - the sword - is the Word of God. That means regular time in the Word daily, and not only when we have an emergency.

18 *praying at all times in the Spirit, with all prayer and supplication. To that end, keep alert with all perseverance, making supplication for all the saints,*

Praying when? At all times in the Spirit, and with ALL prayer and supplication. This means to plead humbly for yourself and others. Always persevere and keep alert!

Putting on the armor of God is important to be able to stand against attacks that come; but watching what we think and what we say is equally important.

Carrie Reichartz

WATCHING OUR WORDS

As I prepare teams to travel across the world with us, we do many things. One of the most important parts of our training is learning and practicing the power of our words. Words are the containers of power that create action. They build up or they tear down. Words have the power to bring life or death physically, emotionally and spiritually. The good news is we have a choice on how to use them.

The triune God shows the power of words when He used them to create the world in the book of Genesis. He then shows us the power of words through Moses when He shared with the Israelites as they were heading into the Promised Land.

> *See, I set before you today life and prosperity, death and destruction.* Deuteronomy 30:15 NIV

The power of our tongue is ruled by our choice. Proverbs 18:21 tells us: death and life are in power of the tongue. Humans are the only ones God gave the power and ability to choose their own words. So we should choose them wisely.

Jesus teaches us that, to tame our tongues, all we need to do is pay attention to what is in our hearts. A good person produces good things from the treasury of a good heart, and an evil person produces evil things from the treasury of an evil heart. What you say flows from what is in your heart (Luke 6:45; Matthew 12:33).

Being filled with Him fills our hearts with life. God also helps us choose life and tame our tongue through the help of the Holy Spirit, which requires time in the Word and prayer.

In more good news, we also have a helper to work with us on this! John 14:26 NKJV shares:

> But the Helper, the Holy Spirit, whom the Father will send in My name, He will teach you all things, and bring to your remembrance all things that I said to you.

One way to help us use our words wisely to build others up. (1 Thessalonians 5:11) To do this we must process the hurt emotions out of our hearts. Psalm 139:22-24 NIV gives us a great testing ground for that:

> Search me, God, and know my heart; test me and know my anxious thoughts. See if there is any offensive way in me, and lead me in the way everlasting.

DECLARE THE VISION & KEEP THE VISION BEFORE YOU

One of the things I'm learning is that it is imperative to not only watch our words but also USE them. We must use our mouth to speak out and declare privately what we hear God moving our vision to and share it with our inside people for amendments and adjustments through prayer. We also need to share that vision out in almost every conversation we have in some small way.

To be able to do that more effectively and avoid attacks the devil throws your way, keep the vision in front of you in photos, pictures, words or whatever reminds you is imperative. It motivates you to work when you don't feel like it. It gets you to share when you're exhausted. Keep the vision before you in words and pictures.

BREACH OF SECURITY!

This book is full of helpful habits and ways to prevent attacks. As you grow, attacks that affect you get less and less because you have your prevention efforts fortified. However, when there is breach of security and you have a situation, here are some words of wisdom from the mission control flight deck!

1. **Open Up And Be Humble About Struggles.**

Cry out to God like the disciples did in the boat in the middle of a storm in Matthew 8. After crying out to Him, it's important to have a safe community space to talk about it.

2. **Christian Community.**

In nonprofit leadership Christian community is critically important. That's where the power is at! That's what makes Christian Rocketeers so special! 1 Corinthians 5:4 ESV tells us:

> *"When you are assembled in the name of the Lord Jesus and my spirit is present, with the power of our Lord Jesus,"*

3. **Difficult Circumstances Close Watch on Words.**

In difficult circumstances, we must watch words even closer. Jesus was silent as He went to the cross; remember this in your darkest struggles.

We need to watch our words but also watch who we are sharing them with! Limit the amount of people you share your struggles with, but don't limit it to 0. You need to have some people you open up to about your struggles. Christ gives us an example of having three close people with you in ministry that you can be open and honest with about what is going on in your head, heart and ministry. (Matthew 17 and many other places.)

4. **Secret Weapons Checklist.**

Below are the "secret weapons" I use in times of distress during a battle and facing extreme opposition. If you're struggling at the moment, this list is a great place to start. We have more specifics in our program.

Have Christian music playing at all times!

Spend more time in the Word!

Give thanksgiving and praise! Dig deep if you have to (food, running water). This will help turn your thoughts about your circumstances around.

Celebrate! Yes, you might not be where you want to be yet, but turn around and celebrate the journey so far. It's important to look how far you have come, so you can be encouraged to keep going.

Pre-praise! Waiting is hard. Praise Him in advance through His promises as you wait.

Pray! Spend time praying and doing what He shares in that time.

Journal! Being real, raw and honest in your emotions to Him in your journal.

Color! Coloring is relaxing and brings peace and discernment especially if those coloring pages include Bible verses.

Create! Whatever that looks like for you - scrapbooking, writing a book, drawing a picture, painting, journaling, etc.

Seek out community/church! Regular church attendance and strong community is vital.

This list is not all inclusive, it's just a starting point. Seek Him and He will lead you to more specific things for you.

PULLING IT ALL TOGETHER

How we respond to opposition reveals our character. Acting with integrity, no matter what the actions of others are, matters.

Faith in God alone is all that will stand the test of time and struggles reveal where you are placing your trust.

Fighting well requires fighting on the right field, the spiritual one. Being in the Word of God, prayer and consistently seeking Him for what and how to take every step. Let's stop just running to Him in the struggles. He will honor our cries of desperation, but He will also help you avoid those pitfalls if we reach out to Him in advance.

Now that you have chosen the right field to fight your battles on; you should also be watching your thoughts and words. You have a checklist when barriers are broken that will help you pick up the pieces.

Next, it's time to start discussing some of the nitty-gritty areas of Christian Rocketeers' nonprofit work. Specifically, how to get systems up and running for funding using our "Five Star Pillars" approach. This approach is our Christian Rocketeer signature: a set-it-and-forget-it nonprofit funding strategy for new nonprofits that sets the stage for financial success. Let's aim for the stars!

CHAPTER 8
SET IT AND FORGET IT FUNDING: OVERCOMING FEAR OF FUNDING

Early in my nonprofit journey, I avoided the title of fundraiser. Taking responsibility for all that was at stake - food, shelter, medical care; the lives of 24-36 girls/babies in Kenya, plus staff- left me feeling overwhelmed and often in tears. Can you relate?

Throughout my journey God has revealed much to me about funding. He has brought me joy and peace. I guess you could say - He brought the "FUN" back to FUNding. He did this by downloading the Christian Rocketeer Five Star signature "set-it and-forget-it" nonprofit funding strategy! Before we lay out this strategy, we have to address and overcome the self funding cycle most nonprofit founders start with.

OVERCOMING SELF FUNDING

I was the only major financial supporter of my own nonprofit for many years. I thought it was an easier and better way. Pride and fear stood in my way of thinking otherwise, although I didn't know it was true at the time.

Fear told me this way I couldn't be rejected. Pride told me, if I self funded, I could control how much was coming in and when. Relying on other people would give me no control.

When God asked me to walk away from my income source, it did not sit well with me. How would I be able to support my nonprofit and my family?

I believed that "I can just work harder and longer. I can do both. I can do more. I don't need to ask other people for help."

However my life reflected a different story. Working harder, longer and faster ended me in the hospital, with relationship difficulties; many balls dropped in my business and my nonprofit.

I remember sitting on a couch in a hotel room at a women's retreat by myself. I couldn't stop trying to figure out a way forward that didn't involve reaching out to other people for help. At that moment, a woman came in and challenged me - "Why will you not ask others for help?"

I shared various excuses, similar to those mentioned above, while crying. She gently exposed the truth. "The real reason you want to do this yourself is pride. It's stopping you from allowing God to bless you. In the process, you are robbing others from the opportunity to join you as the body of Christ." As much as I didn't want to believe it and hated to admit it, she was right.

Is that you right now? Are you self funding your nonprofit? Many of my clients were doing the same thing. Let's figure out a simple "set it and forget it" process for you to invite the body of Christ into your work without it consuming you!

FUNDRAISING STAR 1: Prayer

As you pursue your personal relationship with Christ, He will lead and guide you into ALL that you need in your life and in the life of your nonprofit.

See 2 Corinthians 9:8 NIV:

> *And God is able to bless you abundantly, so that in all things at all times, having all that you need, you will abound in every good work.*

As a type A person and lawyer by trade, it is hard to slow me down. After several years, I finally STOPPED with all the constant "Carrie" and worldly ideas of what I needed to do to make sure my nonprofit ran and was funded. I was CONSTANTLY busy, but my efforts produced very little quality results. But I didn't know any other way. All the conferences I attended - Christian and secular - told me I HAD to do all these things or my nonprofit would not be successful.

This road only leads to burnout. If you don't seek God first before going after funding and anything else in your nonprofit, you will be striving and not abiding. That never ends well for anyone.

It was scary. I didn't know what would happen. It was like a trust fall into the arms of someone behind you. I stopped "doing" and spent more time in prayer instead.

THERE IS NO WAY THIS WILL WORK

At first, praying felt like a HUGE waste of time and initially it didn't look like it would bring in any funding.
I was constantly in front of people doing more fundraisers and constantly asking - even though I was terrified to make the ask for money.

Just like the miracle of manna was to the Israelites, the money started coming; not by doing, but by listening and doing what God called me to do everyday. He brought more vision clarity. He revealed specific ways and places to share that vision. He opened doors to places to share the message, and identified the people who the message was for.

As I obeyed He answered my prayers by bringing all the money and people needed. My part: TRUST HIM. Like astronauts put their faith in mission control, put your faith in Him. As I did, miraculous results started happening!

Do you see how this can bring the FUN back to FUNDING? As we seek Him and ask Him, He provides the results! The phrase "God helps those who help themselves" is not in the Bible and is not Biblical. God helps those that ask and depend on Him for His help. (Genesis 49:25 NIV; Psalm 34:18 NIV)

FUNDRAISING STAR 2: Individuals

Did you know that 70-80% of nonprofit funding comes from individuals? It's not from grants or businesses. Even if you have a program suitable for grant funding - you still cannot have all your funding eggs in one basket. Diversification of funding is imperative for financial stability and to be able to serve your clients well.

If one financial source dries up or wants to control the program in a way you are not comfortable with, you need to have solid bases of support in other areas to be able to weather that storm with ease and grace.

The nonprofit vision is important and the integrity of the organization and the person running the organization are equally important! But, before people will give to your nonprofit, they have to know, like, and trust you. It's a well known truth in business.

That being true, what better place to start than with your family and friends? Even though this is the best place to start, you WILL experience resistance. I shared my emotional resistance story earlier in this chapter. Sometimes this resistance shows up as our own self-talk:

> My "people" won't give.
> You don't know my friends and family.

I'll ask other people for money, but not my friends and family.
I don't want to share what I'm doing with friends and family until it's off the ground.
I'll find other funding sources so I don't need to ask family and friends.

If you identify with any of the above thoughts, know you are not alone. We all think and feel them. Let me encourage you to dig deeper into getting to the emotional roadblock that is keeping you stuck. Usually it's pride or fear, and you must push past it for funding and leadership.

Always remember, God is in charge of bringing the finances. Asking family and friends first is a quick way to push past the emotional, spiritual and mental blocks you have between you and fully funding the organization. It will influence later funding strategies.

The reality is, many WILL give and these are your best sources of funding as you start. Our programs give you templates and assist you in writing effective letters, posts, and other types of funding materials. We also help you determine the best way for you to move forward the quickest.

FUNDRAISING STAR 3: Events

Special events are an amazing avenue to share what you are doing and develop relationships. Events can lead to long-term donors and also passionate, inspired and loyal volunteers. There are simple events and super complicated events; either one can be, if well planned, a great way to bring in money!

If you are a natural organizer or if you have someone on your team who is, you may be drawn to putting on events. I love hosting events and have hosted many widely successful ones; however, I've also had my share of fundraising disasters as well. I could easily share a full course on them!

A word of caution, don't let events take over space that should be used for Fundraising Stars #1 Prayer and #2 Individuals. These fundraising strategies build on each other. As you share with family and friends, there are more people that are likely to show up at your event and you will have some who support the events and others that help organize and run them with you!

Event prep is a speciality of ours and I would love to go on for hours on this topic.

FUNDRAISING STAR 4: Businesses, Churches, & Organizations

These are relationships that take awhile to initiate, form, and build. This is a long-term strategy. Many organizations will want to see substantial individual support and some proven results before joining forces with you.

Start with finding organizations, business, churches with similar goals as your organization. Don't try to force your program into their goals. Either you will have similar goals or you won't. You must be honest with yourself and with them.

We have been blessed to partner with other nonprofits with larger funding bases to do parts of projects. Joyce Meyer Ministries partnered with us to build our Mercy's Light maternity home. We have partnered with local businesses and churches for various funding aspects of our program with great success.

Most organizations prefer a one-time donation, versus an ongoing monthly obligation to start a relationship. Approaching a business or organization asking for a small matching grant and/or event sponsorship is a great start. Then keep conversations going. These partnerships often blossom into deeper connections and relationships. Stewarding these relationships should be the focus.

The Rotary or Lions Clubs and other civic organizations do lots of grants, even internationally.

Carrie Reichartz

NOT ALWAYS A CHARM...NEVER WASTED

It is also important to be ready to invest time and effort and not get the results you hoped for. I remember spending 7+ months working full time attending meetings, developing relationships, writing the proposal, and gathering all the required information working towards a partnership grant from a civic organization.

All of a sudden, six months into this agonizing, overwhelming process, I was made aware that someone was spreading lies about me behind my back. It was a person I had helped with her own organization. She wanted to apply for the same grant for her organization, so she did all she could to make that happen. Besides being deeply hurt, and really needing the money for my nonprofit, I also felt like I completely wasted my time for the last seven months!

After my second day in tears, God sent the check from Joyce Meyer Ministry! We sent a letter several months prior asking for funds with no response (which is very normal). The check appeared without any prior notice that we would be receiving it.

It was a "kiss" from God that showed up at the exact right time when I needed it the most. He used that check to help me to stop focusing on what didn't happen. It helped keep me moving forward. He also revealed for me to stay focused on Christian funding for now. So, though that organizational partnership grant didn't come through, the reality was all the work I did was used for future endeavors.

As you get into business, organization, church and grant funding, prepare your heart for disappointment and know that nothing you do on His calling will ever come back void. (Isaiah 55:11). You may not get that partnership or grant, but, if He called you to the project, and even if He didn't, He will use what you created and will bless you even more for your focus on Him. Time is never wasted with Him, it's redeemed! (Romans 8:28)

FUNDRAISING STAR 5: Grants (optional)

Grants are a long term strategy. Grants are about relationships like businesses, organizations and churches. They are really great for some specific work and not so great of an option with other work.

This "Star" takes time and patience. Finding them is a fulltime job. You can hire people that are experts to search for you, but be very careful. There are people holding themselves out as experts, who aren't. Ask to see their results and verify with the recipient organization that they are valid.

Once you find a grant that makes sense for your nonprofit, you usually send a short letter asking for permission to apply. It's even better if you can find someone you know on the board of the foundation. I recommend you hire an expert to do this and the grant writing for you. It is an art and a science and best left to someone that does it fulltime with proven results.

We have now covered the five star strategies! They can be life changing to you and your nonprofit. If you don't have the proper financial backbone and mindsets, little you do will be effective. Let's get those mindsets cleaned up together!

BACKBONE OF ALL FINANCIAL SUCCESS: TITHING

One rule we started early on in the process of building our nonprofit was tithing (giving 10%) on most of the funds that came into our ministry. Tithing at the beginning was PAINFUL! I didn't have enough money to do the project I KNEW God was calling me to, so how could I give money away that I needed for my nonprofit?

Sitting in the pew at a conference, I became angry as this man shared about an orphanage he was building in Tanzania. Maybe I was annoyed that God hadn't brought the funds for us yet; or jealous that His ministry was so much more successful; even though I had no idea how successful his ministry was.

I went home with these less than pretty thoughts and emotions. The next morning, during my devotional time, it became clear that I was to donate 10% of what we had in our account currently to this man and his project.

I wanted to do no such thing. This command came when NOTHING was happening in our ministry. We had been working for five years and there was not one thing to show for it; no land, no committed team, and not enough finances to do anything. Nothing.

I was asking for money left, right and sideways. I was doing many fundraisers. I was out there. Way out there. Honestly, I was losing hope. Thoughts of "Will this ever happen?" started to surface. Nothing seemed to be moving forward and it appeared to be going backward.

Now, God was telling me to give 10% of my hard earned, nose to the grindstone, money to this program that I didn't have good feelings about anyway. I took the checkbook with me fully intending to bring it home with all the checks still intact. At some point during the conference, the Holy Spirit got a hold of my heart. It was as though He was saying "Carrie, do you trust me?" "Do you trust I can do this?"

Warm tears streamed down my face as I wrote the check for more money than I had personally seen in a long time! Tears of fear. Tears of "When God when". Tears of worry. Tears of hurt. Tears of the wait. Long after I dropped my check into the silver bowl, the tears continued.

A few years later, I realized something. This was the moment that set me free. I was free from fear and the bondage of money. Money had control over me until that point. Tithing is not about the money, it's about your heart. If you are unwilling to give 10% or what God is calling you to give, it's not about the money. It's about the control money has over your heart at that moment. If you are not trusting God, you are trusting in the money. Giving is a physical display of your trust in God, not in the money.

GOD'S USE FOR MONEY

We have distorted money's power and its actual abilities in our minds. We forget money is just paper and metal. God has control over all things in this world and that includes money. He can move it around as He sees fit. We do not need to be a slave to it. Tithing, and specifically joyful tithing, helps us remember that and stay in that mindset! (2 Corinthians 9:7 NIV)

It's through His Spirit that we can accomplish what He has purposed for us. Our power does not come from money, it comes from God and God alone. Ephesians 3:16-17 ESV also shares:

> *that according to the riches of his glory he may grant you to be strengthened with power through his Spirit in your inner being, so that Christ may dwell in your hearts through faith—that you, being rooted and grounded in love,*

God has a use for money and it's for taking care of ourselves, our families and funding kingdom projects as He directs. That is His plan for money. He is clear we cannot serve two masters. We must serve Him. (Matthew 6:24 NIV) If He has called you to a nonprofit His Word will not come back void (Isaiah 55:11) He will provide.

Will you believe in His promises: "fully convinced that God was able to do what he had promised." Romans 4:21 ESV?

Making the painful decision to tithe that day, when I didn't see how I could afford it, pushed me through those lies of not enough, never enough. It brought me to the point of literally crying out to Him and Him showing me where the real power was. In Him. It finally brought me to my knees and I gave the burden for funding this project off of me and onto God; right where it belongs!

Hyperfocusing on finances takes our focus off the vision and mission and what we really need to create a sustainable nonprofit - the people. Let's find out more about that in the next chapter.

CHAPTER 9
PEOPLE: MONEY IS NOT THE MOST IMPORTANT PROVISION

When we think about provision related to ministries, we often only think of financial provision. "If I just had the money everything would be simple and everything else would fall into place."

Yes, money is needed for success: but it is not the most important part. Your relationship with God is your number one key to success. As your relationship with Christ flourishes, He reveals His vision. With boldness and direction, share this vision with the next most important piece of nonprofit work - people!

Being hyper-focused on money was distracting me from the main resource God was providing - Himself and the right people. I would launch 6-12 fundraisers a year and do anything I thought would raise funds. I spent very little time seeking God for guidance.

For 10 years, I developed Mercy's Light Family from the ground up. For many of those years, there was no visible progress. I was convinced money was the only obstacle to providing the amazing services God was calling us to. I was frustrated that God was delaying the process while young girls and babies were dying.

Now, experience, wisdom, knowledge and this scripture and others have changed my mindset. God can handle all the money and the people. Is anything too hard for God? *"Behold, I am the Lord, the God of all flesh. Is anything too hard for me?"* Jeremiah 32:27 ESV

SLOW DOWN & LET HIM BRING THE RIGHT PEOPLE

I learned that my job is not about a to-do checklist. Instead, it is to be obedient. Go when God says go. Stay when He says stay. I focus my life around Him and let Him pull the details together. He does that remarkably well if we let Him. By releasing control over to Him, we see miracle after miracle!

I recently read: disobedience keeps you stuck, obedience sets you on fire. If I choose to push into Him, it means I have control over this pace.

I am a very task/project oriented person. I like seeing my to-do list being checked off. My early trips to Kenya were devoted to developing relationships. I invested thousands of dollars to book a ticket to Kenya in January for a March trip. In Kenya, people generally don't book meetings out more than a day or two. I had to make a flight reservation and hope to set up meetings to see the right people. I had to trust Him in the process and the details.

Since I needed employees, staff and leadership in Kenya and also in the US, I see exactly why God needed the time to pull the right team together to work the vision and mission. God forced me to slow down so I could watch Him work out all the details.

If you are reading this and feel like you are not seeing the fruit of your labor, don't worry. God is moving on your behalf! When God told Abraham to look at the night sky and count the stars. God shared Abraham's descendants would be as numerous as the stars. Abraham's reality did not show that at all. Abraham had no children at the time, but God was working out all the details behind the scenes. Just like He will for you!

RELATIONSHIPS NEEDED

Building a rocket that will launch and sustain itself all the way to the space station and stay there for years takes a solid foundation. It is not a one person job. You need the body of Christ to produce a quality rocket and a space station to support this work! It takes many people (the community you serve, your board, donors, staff, and volunteers) to carry out this mission.

Let's take a look at the most important relationships you will need to grow into a solid, profitable and sustainable nonprofit. If you take anything away from this book take: "Do not do it alone." God calls us to be in community, not to be a lone ranger. We need guidance, direction and accountability from others. We need a "mission control center". Let's explore some parts of that below.

1. **Relationship With God.**

This always remains #1 - your personal time with Him. Once this is established, then you can focus on the goals of your mission.

2. **Mentors: People That Have Gone Before You. Submission.**

This includes: people of authority, coaches and accountability.

You don't know what you don't know. What you don't know could get you or the people you are working with in BIG trouble. Legal, accounting, banking, not to mention marketing, and more expertise is required. Make sure to be submissive to the right people in authority over you along the way.

It's imperative to find other people doing similar work in the area in which you are working. You need to listen, and learn from them. These are your mentors, not coaches. As your mentor, you learn from their mistakes in the specific area geography and specific area of practice.

Jim and Susie Horne are an example of people of authority for me. They started in Kenya in the late 1970's. They raised a family there and learned about the culture and they grew relationships. They laid a beautiful groundwork for all that is happening today and their faithfulness led to the success of Mercy's Light Family! Without them and their long, sometimes lonely, tireless, and at times thankless work, Mercy's Light wouldn't be here today.

The Hornes are not nonprofit experts and they are focused on daily work. They know the local area I am working in and have authority over that area of the work.

3. Key People Of Peace.

People of Peace are people who bring you knowledge of the culture, good local people, the Holy Spirit and so much more. These people should also keep you grounded and focused on Christ as you do the same for them!

You will never be able to get your mission off the ground and sustain it well if you don't first find and work with People of Peace in the local area where you will be working. They can be ambassadors and leaders for you in your program.

People of Peace are mentioned in Luke 10:3-11 and Matthew 10:11-14. Let's walk through Matthew 10 (NIV) together to see why People of Peace are so important for your nonprofit.

Verse 11 Whatever town or or village you enter, search there for some worthy person and stay at their house until you leave.

Enter, search, and stay. Don't keep jumping from person to person. Stay to determine their character, if they have a pure heart towards God, stick with them. This is a Holy Spirit decision, not a human one. Is the Holy Spirit giving you rest/peace about this person?

If yes, let them support you with food and drink. Make the relationship a two-way street of giving and taking. No lopsided power imbalance.

QUESTIONS FOR YOU...

Who is your Person of Peace in the area you are working?

Are you letting them give back to you as you give to them and/or their community? If yes, how?

Do you refuse gifts from them or avoid sharing struggles with them?

Verse 12 *As you enter the home, give it your greeting.*

Open yourself up to them. Tell them, and keep telling them, you want to know the real them. Make sure they are not trying to please, appease or impress you. Keep repeating that you are equal and you want to share openly and have them share openly. Don't hide your heart. As you share your heart, they will share theirs. Give it time.

QUESTIONS FOR YOU...

Honestly describe your relationship. Do you listen to personal things from your Person of Peace? Or is your relationship more a to-do list?

Do your People of Peace know it's okay to say no to you? Do you remind them of that often?

How have you shared your heart to your People of Peace recently?

How long has your relationship been with your Person of Peace? Are you allowing it to unfold naturally over time? Are you trying to force it to make things move faster?

Verse 13(a) *If the home is deserving, let your peace rest on it;*

Is their character, value and heart consistent? If you share vision and mission then continue with the relationship... Let your heart and peace rest on them as theirs rests on you.

For me this first and foremost means sharing the gospel and then caring well for my girls and babies and staff at Mercy's Light Family.

QUESTIONS FOR YOU...

What is the heart character of your Person of Peace? What is the vision and mission they see God putting on their life? Is that consistent with your work?

Verse 13(b) *if it is not (deserving), let your peace return to you.*

Don't try to force this person to be someone they are not. Don't deceive yourself into thinking they are something they are not. Don't freak out. Don't stress out. Don't try to force it to work because you've invested time and/or money into this person. Take your peace and carry on. God will bring the exact right person.

QUESTIONS FOR YOU...

Is there any area where you are convincing yourself this is your Person of Peace, but there are signs suggesting otherwise?

Are you trying to force this onto someone or are you trusting God with this process?

***Verse 14** If anyone will not welcome you or listen to your words, leave that home or town and shake the dust off your feet.*

You are called to be obedient. Their reaction does not need to affect you. Leave and bring your hurting heart back to Christ and move on. Don't sit in guilt and don't try to force something to work when it is not His will. Just keep moving with Him.

QUESTIONS FOR YOU...

Check your motives? Will being obedient to what God is calling be enough for you? Or do you need everyone to like you and be happy with you as well?

In what areas do you need to bring your hurting heart back to Christ?

WHERE TO FIND THEM

I had a few people of peace along the way until God brought us the one to bring this movement forward. So don't be disappointed if you work for a while with someone and then He moves you to the next person.

For me, my current and hopefully last person of peace is Jocelyne. A mutual friend connected us when she posted on social media looking for a home for a pregnant girl she was working with in her part time ministry. Several months later we had a quick meeting. Then another. Then another. Then another. Now we chat almost daily and she is our person of peace. I share this to say you don't find them. He brings them to you. Be open, aware, and pursue relationships (with Him and people) not tasks.

4. Community Recipients

When working in a community different from where you grew up and/or live, your first priority is not bringing them what YOU think they need. Your first priority is to meet, talk with, listen to, and create solutions WITH the community you plan to serve.

Do not, for any reason, build a program you feel will fill a need or a void without getting into relationship with people living and working in whatever area God is calling you to. When we do, our "help" can actually hurt.

This is a major problem in nonprofits today. Please be very careful. It is often very subtle and can be difficult to detect. This is another reason why having a coach, mentor, and relationships in the area is critical!

5. Coaches

Looking back, I wish I had invested in coaching long before I finally did. It would have kept me focused, accountable, and actually doing the right things; not just spinning in circles being busy. It would have cleared away the confusion and prevented several missteps along the way and saved me a ton of time and money.

6. Board Members

To have Holy Spirit, rocket-fueled success, you will need two boards: a traditional governance board and a separate prayer board.

Our governance board will challenge us. They will have specific skill sets that we don't have that will help the mission and vision grow.

Your prayer board will uplift, encourage and be there for you as a prayer warrior with the Holy Spirit and Christ (Romans 8) as you regularly communicate with them in person, by phone or email.

We address a lot more of the specifics regarding board members and boards in our Christian Rocketeers course and programs. They are a critical piece to your mission.

7. Volunteers/Staff

Volunteers are amazing and we praise the day they arrive because we don't have to do it alone anymore! But we can become quickly disappointed. Having volunteers does not mean you don't have to do anything. Similar to bringing a new employee into a business, it takes awhile to learn the systems and culture to be fully independent. Your work can become more complicated in the short run. We will talk more about this in the next chapter on leading and managing your nonprofit.

We have found key volunteers through people that cared enough about our cause to attend events. We had lunch and now they are long term committed donors.

On the Kenyan side - we needed a new social worker for our project. We sat down and had prayerful conversations with a friend of the project. Randomly a person she had worked with through Compassion International came into her mind. She had only run into her through her work a few times at corporate events. She reached out. We did an interview. We hired her a few days later.

Other hires came through facebook posts asking and then interviewing. The key to interviewing and finding the right people - hire based on their relationship with God, they can learn the skill you need.

8. Donors

Donors are the blood that keeps the body flowing. They are critically important to the success of your nonprofit. You need to know who your donors are and where they hang out. Then you need to know what and how to share and speak with them effectively. This is very specific to your

Rocket Your Nonprofit

nonprofit area and is something we cover a lot in our courses and coaching at Christian Rocketeers.

God wants to build something through you that will last. He's expanding the table for the right people. He wants to be invited to the table so the work is sustainable over the long haul. He's not in a hurry to build just to watch it quickly crumble under the wrong people. Go slow and let it take its time to build with the right people.

Now that you know the type of people you need for your nonprofit, let's figure out where to find them, and how to best manage and lead them! See you in the next chapter!

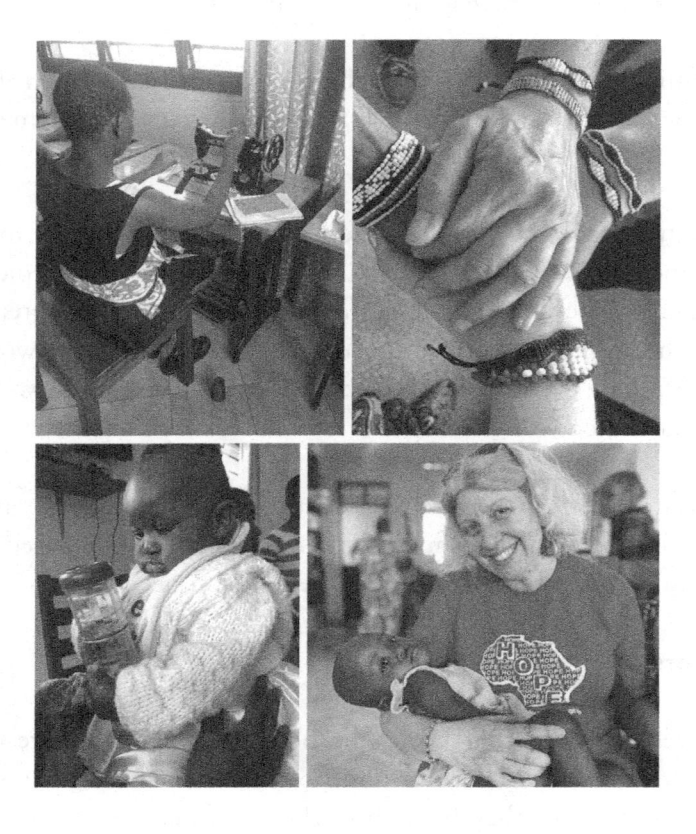

CHAPTER 10
TRUSTING, LEADING, & FINDING YOUR PEOPLE

The hardest part about working with people is remembering that we are people! All of us are flawed, mistake makers, hurtful thing sayers, disappointers, etc. Certain people reveal our own flaws and it's not easy to handle. It leads us to want to isolate ourselves and do everything on our own. God does not work in isolation - He's a group project kind of guy! He will empower and enable us as His chosen leaders to navigate whatever comes up with people being so "peoplie"! Let's look at some Biblical examples, take a crash course on how to best manage and lead people and also figure out where to find your people.

EXPECT DISAPPOINTMENT - PAUL, BARNABAS AND JOHN MARK

Even Paul, the writer of most of the New Testament, had relationship struggles with the people he worked with. Acts 15:36-41 shares an argument that brought hardship between Paul and his right hand man, Barnabas. They were fighting about John Mark, who Paul felt deserted them on a previous missionary journey. There was so much friction they parted ways.

I'm sure this division brought a deep heartache to Paul. I can relate to this as I've had my share of those heart wrenching divisions. God will work out the details as you trust in Him, and not people.

In Paul and Barnabas' case, their division brought more of God's work to two different parts of the world. Paul went one way with his team and Barnabas and John Mark went another way, so more of the world got the Gospel faster.

Though John Mark may have deeply wounded Paul, Paul affectionately mentions John Mark in a later letter. That is thought to be the same Mark that wrote the Gospel of Mark. This is what Romans 8:28 looks like in action. He works ALL things out!

TRUST GOD NOT PEOPLE: WORKING AS THE BODY OF CHRIST

Trust is hard, especially when you have been disappointed along the way of life and along the way of ministry. That's why we spent so much time in earlier chapters dealing with early hurts in our lives; so we can be more effective leaders now. As we talked about in previous chapters, taking our emotions to God is critical in working with people and especially when heartache comes. Sometimes that means pushing through it and continuing in the relationship, allowing God to bring healing to your heart, or it means it's time to part ways, even when it may feel unchristian like to move on. Some relationships may pause for a while, but we can be open in the future if God brings the relationships back together. Staying connected to Him and what He has for you is key to your nonprofit success.

In my journey, there were a few people I thought were the exact right people to move the project forward; when I was honest with myself, I was pushing my will more and depending on the Holy Spirit less. As I did, nothing, or at least very little, was happening. Sometimes things even moved backward.

I desperately wanted some of them to be the right people. I wanted to start the work of saving the babies and moms in Kenya. I didn't want any more girls or babies to suffer and wanted to get the work started ASAP. The time I spent forcing relationships with people that weren't from God was a waste of time and money. God will not move forward with the wrong people. Once the right people were at the table, things sky-rocketed faster than I would have liked.

Slow down. Ask Him to reveal to you if these are the right people. Let Him bring the right people. Start taking baby steps. Seek God together and be willing to follow His will. Then you will see miracles! Now, how do we get there and what are some steps to avoid?

LEADERSHIP/MANAGING

For a Christian, leadership has 3 main areas:

1. Personal Development - your identity in Christ and not stepping outside of that.

2. Christian Values - walking out that identity in relationship to others - through humility, submission, obedience, working as a body, loving, forgiving, and faith.

3. Logistics of Leading - lead, conflict resolution, organization development and management.

We spent time in earlier chapters on #1 & 2 so let's focus on a few of #3.

TO LEAD OR NOT TO LEAD, THAT IS THE QUESTION

Stepping into your leadership is critical. I bowed to other people's thoughts and opinions for too many years. I didn't take the reins as a leader. There is a time and place for shepherding your people, but it is not how you lead the organization. Shepherding should be done in your private one-on-one time. First lead the organization, then shepard.

An example of how I was shepherding and not leading was my management of volunteers. The temptation I fell into over and over was taking anyone who wanted to help; even if the mission doesn't need that type of volunteer at the moment.

Spending time creating opportunities that God might not be calling for right now just to ensure volunteers are used is harmful to your organization. Instead, take it to prayer and ensure God is calling you to use that volunteer right now. When in doubt, the answer should be no. Stay focused on the next right step, which means not creating projects for volunteers just to use them. You need to ensure you are leading the organization in the way God is calling you to.

This was very difficult for me and maybe for you as well. I still occasionally struggle with it. I want everyone to be able to be a part. To say "not at this time", when someone wants to be a part of it, is HARD.

This style of leadership ensures and forces you to be in prayer in general about your "mission" but also about the "specifics" of what is next and how God wants you to get there. It is an outward example of true dependence on Him.

I had similar pitfalls with setting up my board. I wanted everyone to be included in every decision. I wanted to have a large board and the exact right people on it as we were just getting started. The reality is a small organization needs a small board to be able to move quickly. As you grow the board will grow with you.

Yes we want to stay in humility, but we also need to take the authority He has given us by appointing us as leaders over this vision and mission. We should make a list of needed volunteer and paid positions through prayer. And then continue in prayer with Him on where to find the people to fill those. Stand strong in your authority in Christ in working with volunteers, donors, and staff.

HAVE THE TOUGH CONVERSATIONS

If one person is fighting with everyone and has a toxic personality and brings strife, don't let it sit and hope it will get better. It is your job as the leader to manage that person and point out their behavior in a kind and loving way. Hopefully it will change their entire life. They may be angry and hurtful back to you, but, whatever the outcome, it is your job to handle these situations as the Bible outlines. Don't let strife fester, even if it appears to have resolved itself without your involvement.

It will always come back! Deal with it straight out. Air it out one-on-one with the person. You don't need to get worked up about this. Make it a conversation; ask the person what is going on. Then you can take it to the group they are directly involved with together.

Don't be afraid to let people go. If you have a person that volunteered to do graphic arts work, but they never complete the projects, don't be afraid to let them go. The temptation is to hold on to someone because at least that person is there in name. The reality is, if they aren't doing the work, they aren't there for the mission. Our minds trick us into thinking we have the role filled with a name, so somehow, there is peace and calm in that. The reality is, it's actually more frustrating and God cannot fill the role with the right person until the person that is currently in it is removed. It also will bring your morale and the morale of healthy team members down.

WHERE TO FIND PEOPLE

By now you may be thinking, "That's great Carrie, I need these people. Where am I supposed to find them?"

Great question! Christian Rocketeers' spends a lot of time helping our client's through this process. It's critical to get it right. If you get the wrong people in, it will set you back in the work: emotionally, spiritually and potentially even financially. So don't rush this and make sure you are working with someone on the process. While our coaching services and courses cover this more in depth, here is a short checklist to get you started:

1. Relationship With God

This has been discussed all throughout this book.

2. Mentors

One of my people of peace - Jocelyne is not local to the area of Kenya. She's from another area of the country. I met her through a western-style church I attend regularly while in Kenya. A fellow friend connected us because of our missions. She does outreach to commercial sex workers and she had a client who was pregnant. She is a person of peace because of her skills and personality.

I had no idea, when we met in November of 2016, on a hard bench outside the church, a few short years later she would be like a sister to me! It all started sharing together what God was calling us to and then walking that out together day by day. Walking together, to see where God was leading us, and then both being willing to take the next step of trust with God at the center.

As a side note for international nonprofits: Befriend and connect with the local rural church. Also find a western style church that you can attend regularly and aligns with your values and doctrine. Most of our staff come from western style churches. This will be a great place for consultancy on local issues as well as gaining valuable staff. One place to start looking for this type of church is in, or nearby, the biggest closest city to you.

3. People Of Peace

See questions in the last chapter that lead you through this process.

If you are working in a foreign country or an area of the city or country you do not live in; you will need to spend focused time on praying and finding people of peace in the area you are working in. This takes time, and research, lots of questions and listening. Give it the time and attention it deserves. Don't rush this. Meet with anyone that will meet with you in the area God is calling you to. Ask them for recommendations and advice and more people to meet with. Keep going.

You've searched for them, but you don't lull them in. Let them come to you through strong vision and mission. Their relationship with Christ and their passion for the vision is the most important part of this. If you are in agreement on these two things, the rest of the details will work themselves out.

Money and what you bring can create power imbalance and also create false motives. Be very careful, especially in developing countries, to find these people before the money starts flowing. Test out their character and trustworthiness slowly. They should bring a great relationship with Christ to the table and knowledge of the local community and commitment.

4. **Community Recipients**

This is more a part of vision and mission. After these are settled, this will be obvious.

5. **Coaches**

We are here! Find out more info at the back of the book.

6. **Board**

What is your vision and mission? Are you communicating it clearly?
What skills are you looking for? Be clear on this and the people will surface.
Who do you know that owns a business?
Where do you do business that someone might be willing to serve?

7. **Volunteers**

What is your vision and mission? Are you communicating that clearly?
Do you have your 501(c)(3) tax exemption letter from the IRS? Try VolunteerMatch.org.
Have you connected with college campuses for fraternities, courses and internship possibilities? Also certain beauty pageantry organizations are great places to find motivated volunteers.
Never ignore family, friends and public social media requests.

8. Donors

What is your vision and mission? Are you communicating that clearly?
Are you just jumping in with your needs first?
Are you clearly outlining your needs and what it will take to get them met?
Are you being honest in your handling of the finances and following God's principles of finance?
Have you taken time to determine the ideal donor for your organization?
Are you hanging out where your ideal donor is hanging out?
Are you sharing your success stories?
Are you sharing things for people to know, like and trust you? Or just needs?

MISSION CONTROL CENTER

It takes a "mission control center" to raise up a project that God is calling you to. That's why He says it's the body of Christ.

It takes time to build relationships to support your mission. Building the right relationships doesn't happen overnight. People take time to reveal their true purpose and intentions. In turn, it will also take time for you to find their highest skill set and value to the organization. Don't rush it.

If you try to rush rocket building or space station development, you will be sadly disappointed and have to start again and there could be devastating losses along the way. I suffered through those losses. I learned the hard way. Using Christian Rocketeers as your coach to walk you through the process will be much faster and easier. Having a solid foundation is the key to a nonprofit that will last!

Rocket Your Nonprofit

Don't be discouraged if it doesn't always work out with people you trusted. Relying on people strengthens our trust. Our trust in people, yes; but more so our trust in God. The bottom line is people will disappoint you, but you are relying on God not your community or volunteers. Let's work together to get the right people in place for your nonprofit and avoid as much of that as possible. If and when it does happen, remember, God is in control not a key volunteer/staff person, donor, or even you!

Now that you know how important people are, even more important than finances, you will spend proper time and attention shepherding your people and finding the right people and putting them in the right place. You know which roles you need to fill and find people for and we have ideas and questions to start looking for them.

As you steward your people well, miracle after miracle will start to happen. Let me not tell you, let me show you in the next chapter.

CHAPTER 11
MERCY'S MIRACLES MOMENTS: LESSONS FROM ALONG THE WAY

I cannot begin to share all the miracles God has done spiritually, emotionally, financially, mentally, and educationally, through Mercy's Light Family. Below are a few that we see everyday (all the names have been changed to protect identities).

I share these for a few reasons:

*To show examples of how the Holy Spirit works in practical ways.

*To encourage you and bring you hope that He did it for us and He will do it for you too!

Don't use these as an example to copy exactly what we did. That won't bring you the results or the peace you are looking for. You need to seek the Holy Spirit and do what He is calling you to specifically do.

STARTING SOMEWHERE: BABY STEPS OF OBEDIENCE

Before we had a facility, we needed to start doing something to build momentum in the Kenyan community as well as stir interest in donors. As a need came before us in an area God was calling us to, we would work to meet that need. Here is one such story:

When "Brittany" was a junior in high school, she was raped and impregnated. Her baby "Iris" is now 2 years old. Her Grandma allowed her to stay in the home and is attempting to care for the baby. Thanks to a sponsor who provides her with educational funds, Brittany is finishing school. Also, thanks to a college student who donated $50, grandma was set up with a small fish drying business.

I share this story to show you won't start with the full vision of your project right away. But are you willing to start somewhere? Take baby steps.

WHERE WILL YOUR VISION AND MISSION COME FROM?

We received the vision and mission for Mercy's Light from God through prayer. Literally sitting on the couch every morning, and sometimes throughout the day, praying and asking God what He wants and how He wants me to do it.

I took many detours - thinking I had great plans for raising the money or great ideas of what the program should look like. We looked at other things that were out there for guidance; but, in the end it was my one-on-one time with God that raised up this mission and its effective, strategic and funding plans.

VISION/MISSION EVOLUTION AND IMPORTANCE OF SELF CARE

We started with a very complicated vision and mission statement which shared all the details of what we would be doing for our girls and the community. We found that people were overwhelmed when they read it and didn't understand it and were not drawn to the complicated details.

God led us to something much simpler: Mercy's Light: A Light In The Darkness

This statement came to me while I was getting a massage. One thing God taught me through this journey was I needed to care for myself, as well as my clients. One way for me to avoid sickness was to get regular massages. At the beginning I didn't see how I could afford it. It was very difficult to "waste" the funds on luxury. But, as I did it, He brought all the funds for it and brought knowledge I needed through it!

Mercy's Light brings the hope that God's love will light the way in the darkest of times! We do this in a variety of ways. Now the hard part is staying there and not finding new bright shiny things. We get bored with using the same language all the time. It's the consistency that leads to donors seeing and knowing you. We cannot keep changing even though we get bored by it. It's out brand just like McDonalds uses "I'm loving it". We need to stick with the same message over and over and over. It's said in different and exciting ways, but the message remains the same.

CORE VERSES

Early on, as I was reading through the Bible for the first time, the following verses in Isaiah 61 kept rising up off the page. As God began downloading the Mercy's Light vision/mission and details, He brought Isaiah 61:1-3 to light as our core verse through prayer.

What's your core verse? Pray and ask Him. Use your verse as guidance when you want to add a new program or close down a program or take on a certain client or activity. Does it fit within your core verse?

EXPANSION OF PROGRAMS - HOW AND WHY:
MERCY'S LIGHT TRANSFORMATIONAL TRANSITION HOUSE EXPANSION: SEEING A NEED

Mercy's Light first started doing work in the community with pregnant girls. Then we bought property, built a wall, built a building and started running a 3-year maternity home program. Miracle after miracle was involved in all of that. Some of which has been shared in the earlier financial chapter.

After doing this work for four years we noticed a DEEP need.

Many of our girls, because of various family situations, don't have parents to go back to. Some are orphans when they arrive. Some have been abused by members of their own family. Some are rejected simply because of the pregnancy. Others are close to 18 when they arrive so leave the program early due to age.

To help these girls and keep them safe as they transition from our home into becoming self-supporting, we discovered a desperate need for *Transformational Transitional Housing*.

This is approximately a 6-month program. During the first month the girls cover their food expenses. Each month after that, a little more responsibility is added. Rent will be added until they are paying full rent for a safe place in the community to stay. This shows us and them they are able to move on safely.

UPDATE: Although this program has been successful for some girls, it has not been successful for all girls. We don't hide this from our donors. We ask our donors for feedback. We share how we are attempting to amend the program to meet more needs. We ask for prayers and pray asking God how to improve on this program daily, and then implement the changes He is calling us to.

Carrie Reichartz

HOW TO TAKE ON EXPANDED VISION - DREAM - COUNTING THE COSTS
MERCY'S LIGHT COMMUNITY INCOME DEVELOPMENT PROJECTS EXPANSION

Our Kenyan Mercy's Light manager had a vision to start income generating businesses using products readily available. A short time later someone from the university approached her about a coconut project they were hoping to launch on the coast. Did you know 5+ products can be made from 1 coconut?

After a year of investigation and prayer we recruited 6 women from the village of Vipingo to train, employ, and empower in this project. We started with an intense one-week training and then six months of tea and Bible study to get our hearts right and to make sure we had the right people in the project, who were not in it just for the money but also the love of the work and sharing of Christ.

We did not jump on day one of this idea. We spent one year praying about it fast and doing baby steps of investigation. We brought it to the team and we brought it to the Lord in prayer. We sought outside opinions and took those to the Lord in prayer. When we finally started the project, we implemented a Bible study during the first one hour of EVERY day of production.

We had our share of difficulties. After money came into the equation, four women had to be removed from the project. That was not fun, but because we had counted the cost, we knew God was fighting the battles for us, so we didn't have to do it. We just needed to walk in obedience and not doubt.

Now we have Frieda and Liz who LOVE the work they do and do it with incredible perfection and joy in spite of receiving very little pay. I love seeing their spirit of wanting to help others in the village by expanding their work and doing it with diligence. Frieda is so grateful for the donors and also the skill she can share with her children and use to bring in income to pay school fees. Liz is growing in the lord everyday and they go to each other for prayers over their families and communities.

Make sure to count the cost (take stock of everything, gather numbers, ask people, and take it to God before for leading and guidance) and then trust Him in the journey. Let Him fight the battles for you.

These are just two examples of "yes" to expanded vision. I could share hundreds of examples of needs that I wasn't called to meet but were brought before me. Many times it seemed like just the right opportunity at the perfect time that it had to be from God.... but it wasn't. It was the devil in there with distractions and trying to make things look good.

Just because it looks like God ordains something to be "this" perfect it, doesn't mean it is Him.

Be careful, slow and clear. Count the cost and test out the waters with the Holy Spirit and take baby steps before moving forward on new ventures.

JOIN JESUS IN THE WORK HE IS DOING: DON'T CREATE YOUR OWN IDEAS

Recently we launched a new community program in Kenya. For two years God was telling us: "discipleship is key" and "empower women in the community".

Finally, in November 2022 we went to the women's Bible study group in Vipingo to ask them what they saw as their biggest needs and best way to do these two things.

We had a great meeting that was in line with and expanding on what God was already sharing with us: helping women discover and start living their God-given purpose through literacy and discipleship.

Our plan was to roll something out over the next few years. This was just research time.

As the leader of the local church, I met with the pastor to make him aware of our discussions. As we shared with him, he indicated God laid on his heart to do the same thing. He was already collecting food and was preparing to start in a few weeks.

This was a sign to us that God was already at work in Vipingo on this topic and it was an invitation for us to join Him. So we put other plans on hold and spent many hours via video calls and What's App messages. Teacher Charles took charge of the literacy angle. He pulled 2 other teachers in because the turn out was so high. We had a few hiccups with the spiritual component but we got the women's local bible study to come alongside us and we launched the Vipingo Women's Empowerment: Literacy, Discipleship Program just a few months later.

Ninety women enrolled; 3-5 more women come daily wanting to get involved, after 4 months 60 people are consistently coming 3-5 days a week.

Women are on fire and eager to learn to read and write. Women who are over 50 years old are participating. The women are learning about the Word of God and living that out in their lives. There is a revival going on in Vipingo through this women's program.

What if we had waited and didn't join Him in His work in His timing?

Originally this was supposed to be a longer term project for us. We thought we would start it in a few years when we had another staff member on the ground in the city full time. Instead, God was at work and calling us to join Him NOW! We amended OUR plans to be obedient to His.

Join Him in what He is already doing! Do not start your own thing in your own timing.

RUNNING A NONPROFIT IS HARD… TAKE THE TIME TO ENJOY EVEN THE SMALL SUCCESSES….

Day to day life is hard in a nonprofit. You are helping people at their deepest level of need. Emotions run high and money runs low. It's imperative that you celebrate every small victory. Celebrating small wins leads to bigger wins.

WATCH CLOSELY TO SEE WHAT GOD IS DOING AND SHARE IT OUT!
MIRACLE STORIES OF THE GIRLS IN MERCY'S LIGHT FAMILY: EMILY'S STORY

Imagine being a young teen and your mom asks you to deliver some product she sells to a person. You arrive with the product and the man forces you to have sex with him. As it turns out, the product the man bought from your mom was YOU. Sex trafficking at the hands of your own mom. Now you're pregnant and your mom kicks you out of the home. You are alone on the streets to fend for yourself. AFRAID is an understatement!

Through Mercy's Light Family Emily went through intensive spiritual development, and counseling for psychological trauma counseling, living with a loving staff around her and participating in empowering skills programing.

There was a point where she was not feeding her baby and was suffering from deep depression. Our team on the US side was deep in prayer over her. Those on the Kenya side took her to a doctor to help her learn the importance of her role in the baby's life and also to administer to her emotional status.

Miraculously, immediately after prayer and that appointment, Emily overcame her depression. She shares that our loving care, prayers, and the conversation with the doctor that day helped her realize how much Jesus loved her. She has become a whole new person - trusting, learning, and becoming the kindest and hardest worker.

FOLLOWING A SYSTEM TAKES TIME AND PATIENCE

I share the following example to demonstrate you can change a culture one situation at a time. Don't go about changing the culture; go about changing the life of one person. As you do, the culture will change.

Motorbike drivers are notorious for taking advantage of young girls as they give them rides to school. Here are the direct words of our social worker:

I took a motorbike to the center yesterday and, while I was giving directions to where I was going, the boda boda (motorbike) driver opened up that he participated in the construction of the new 3rd floor.

He saw our girls and got to hear what happens there. Apparently he was dating a school age girl whom he had been warned about.

He then made a decision to stop the relationship and asked the girl to focus on education. And that's how he stopped seeing young girls.

He said: "Whenever I see this place, I thank God because it made me realize I was not doing a good thing."

Then I saw God working through MLF in changing lives around the community. So brethren, be encouraged to continue serving. Be blessed!

God is changing the culture one person at a time.

KAY'S STORY

God shared a vision with me early in this journey: "it's not my job or my staff's job to change this community". It's not our community, it's our girls' community. It's their job to change it.

We stand in the gap to let them know and empower them to be strong enough to do that!

Here is one example of that:

After having to prepare for court six separate times, Kay was finally able to testify against her father. Kay was sexually assaulted by her dad and became pregnant. Her father was convicted as a result of his crime and was sent to prison.

Unfortunately, her mom and other family members are not supportive of her or the baby, accusing her of lying and making it all up.

Kay was strong, courageous and brave in court - we are so proud of her for that! Later that day, when she realized ALL her family rejected and abandoned her, she was a crying heep on the lap of Mercy's Light's volunteer manager.

Even some educated judges and lawyers in the community think rape and sexual abuse of your daughter is fine. She's your property; you can do what you want. I'm so glad for judges that do uphold the laws and are changing the world and I'm glad for girls like Kay and our staff who hold those accountable that need to be.

Now Kay knows she has the strength and courage to make a difference in her community and the world around her.

KAY'S STORY PART II: FORGIVENESS

A few months later, Kay had a few more interviews with government officials asking her what her father's sentence should be. She indicated with a confidence, courage, and contentment that astounded the probation officer. "I have forgiven my father and the court system will need to decide what the best sentence is for what he has done." He received 9 years in prison.

Kay now knows the power she has because Christ is inside her. When she leaves Mercy's Light she is now a light to other girls in trouble. She is a light to the court system about how not to do things. She is a light to the probation officer showcasing forgiveness in deep circumstances.

SPIRITUAL TRANSFORMATIONS ARE THE MOST IMPORTANT

In Kenya we are bombarded daily by very basic, desperate needs for water, food, and education. It is very difficult to keep first things first. It is hard to remember and see the only real need is for EVERYONE, myself and those around me, is a spiritual need for Jesus.

It is imperative we remember that and pour into spiritual needs above all else. The physical and emotional healing we do is to pull the girls closer to spiritual healing. Spiritual healing is not optional. It is the most important. Keep that in mind and it will help you not to over focus on the physical. Meeting spiritual needs are much cheaper and more impactful than meeting physical needs. As we keep our focus on the spiritual needs, He will supply all the funds needed for the physical needs He is calling us to meet.

This is true of our clients, our staff, our volunteers and ourselves! Matthew 6:33.

EXAMPLES OF HOW WE DO THIS….

After a trip to Kenya in the fall of 2021, I wrote the following in my blog. TRANSFORMATION.

During a November day - 9 girls were baptized and a week later one more girl gave her life to Christ. So far, every girl who has entered Mercy's Light has chosen to be a part of the body of Christ and that is not taken lightly by our spiritual staff. They are expected to show life change before it is determined they are ready for the next steps toward baptism. In addition to those steps, most girls have also chosen to be baptized despite tremendous cultural fear of the water by many.

WHEN THINGS DON'T WORK - THE HOLY SPIRIT IS STILL THERE

"Linda" was one of the first girls to join our program! Unfortunately, Linda was not applying herself and was not utilizing our program. After five months of counseling her, issuing multiple warnings, being strong with her, and everything else we could think of, Linda went back to her family home which was not a good situation, although it was safe.

We kept in touch with Linda and supplied formula for her baby until her 1st birthday. We watched her move living arrangements several times from mom to dad to brother and sister-in-law. We also lost touch with her for a little while.

Finally, one day, one of our staff saw her in a store. She was shopping for clothes for her daughter. This was strange because food would be the most important need to fill and clothes would be last on the list.

We learned Linda found a job working at a construction site. She had her own place to live with her baby so it was more stable and was even able to afford clothing for her child. She even saved money and was able to assist her father financially with medical bills. She has also been assisting her mom with emotional and mental health issues. She was also enrolling her baby in a private school!

Although we had to let her go from the program, which was emotionally, spiritually and in many ways devastating to us, the Holy Spirit went with her and guided her every step of the way to get her to this point; a place she may not have gotten to without the time she spent in our program.

She returned to Mercy's Light to visit with the current girls and shared how grateful she was for Mercy's Light and how disappointed she was in herself for not taking full advantage of all that was offered. According to her - without Mercy's Light, she and her baby would not be alive today!

The lesson we have clung to, numerous times, as we had to make similar heartbreaking decisions is that the Holy Spirit goes with our girls even when their time in our program must end for one reason or another.

IMPORTANCE OF HEALING
HURTING HEARTS & EMOTIONS

"Lydia's" mom passed away during her stay with us. It happened just one week after the delivery of her baby. Her mom had been with her at the delivery of her baby and the loss broke Lydia's heart and she became depressed. Our trauma counselor, Chou, counseled the girls via zoom from the US during COVID. After beginning her time with Chou, within two months after losing her mom, Lydia was sharing hope with the girls.

She was getting up at 3:00 am so she could read the Word and pray to heal her heart. Winnie, our social worker, overheard her counseling the other girls about not taking their parents for granted as she would do anything for more time with her mom.

After a court case against the man that assaulted her and getting him removed from her community, her family was VERY eager to have her return to them at their home just after Christmas 2020. She was with us about 7 months and she also found her strength in Christ; that she will have for the rest of her life!

Thanks to the support of our donors Lydia and Baby F are doing well and are safe as a family unit together. Lydia's biggest takeaway from Mercy's Light is learning about the Word of God and how Chou worked with her to deal with her emotional pain of losing her mother.

As a nonprofit leader, Lydia is a great example. We must work through our emotional messes. Leaving emotional baggage inside brings hurt and pain to our organization, clients, and people around us.

Don't let your emotions lash out in anger or stuff them down and pretend they don't hurt. Take them to God through journaling and prayer. Get yourself to a counselor when needed. Get a coach or mentor. Read God's Word, especially the Psalms, to find healing and wholeness so you can bring that to your clients.

TRUSTING HIS VISION NOT YOUR WANTS

When I first started this vision and mission, I didn't want to work with teenage moms. I wanted to work with babies. I have loved babies since childhood. I wanted to build a traditional orphanage full of babies! But God had other plans. His vision was for me to work with teen moms who have been through abuse. Though not an easy population to minister to (hormones, trauma, rebellion) I submitted to His plans.

As it turns out - God gave me exactly what I wanted and needed. In a traditional orphanage babies grow up and they take up space so new babies cannot enter. With the way He has us working our program at Mercy's Light Family, we always have babies around because every three years our moms rotate out to start their lives and a new round of young moms and babies come in.

Submit to His plans... He will give you the delight of your heart. You don't want to move forward on something that is not from Him. Trust Him, walk out what He calls you to and let Him leave you in shock and awe!

REACTING TO DEVASTATING NEWS

We spent two years negotiating with a man who owned property right next door to our current property. It was the only property that connected to the current property.

We were just about to close the deal - half payment payable in December and half payment was due in April. In mid-November the property owner called us IRATE! "The deal is off!"

In that moment we had two choices: walk away devastated and fall into an emotional spiral or, walk away remembering if this property is meant for us, God will work out the details; asking Him - does He have something for me to learn? Or change?

As we prayed, we realized we needed to do the full deal at one time, not two separate payments; however, we didn't have the money to do that. We went back to God in prayer. We reached out by email, social media, family and friends. Within two weeks, we had the extra $15,000 we needed to do the full deal in December.

We did all this after a phone call outlining the deal was off. We didn't wait. Two weeks later the property owner reached out to us. He shared he was having a really bad day the day he called and canceled the deal. He was sorry and would like to continue the deal! Now we had all the money we needed and the deal closed shortly thereafter!

I could go on and on with all the crazy faith moments. The point of this example is: do you trust YOURSELF, PEOPLE AND MONEY or do you trust GOD? This is one example of hundreds! God will do it for you too!

CHAPTER 12
WHERE DO WE GO FROM HERE?

So there you have it! I hope you have enjoyed the 10,000 foot view of how God led and directed the build of a Christian profitable nonprofit serving Him and the women and girls of Vipingo, Kenya through Mercy's Light Family!

As I shared in the introduction, after all the lessons learned from this road, God has now brought us to launching Christian Rocketeers to rocket people into their purpose of changing the world by equipping them to start and fund the nonprofit ministry God is calling them to with ease and grace!

In the Christian Rocketeers community, I see many things shift for ourselves and our clients. We start:

*Living out our God-given purpose which is invigorating and inspiring to others around us.

*Soaring spiritually as we connect with God more, full of joy, peace, love more than ever before.

*Living a secure life in our identity in Christ, not our work, and staying emotionally grounded.

*Financially soaring because what He calls us to, He funds including our own care, families and the work.

*Believing and seeing we have all the people and skills we need to bring His vision visibility.

Do you need to take the action God is calling you to? Join the Christian Rocketeers Community!

WHAT ARE OTHERS SAYING?

Don't take my word for it. Here is what one of our clients Georgia had to share:

> *I came to a point in my life where I was asking myself, "Who are you?" Outside of being a survivor, a mother and grandmother I really didn't know who I was or what I enjoyed doing. Although I had been saved for many years, I was not actively seeking God or his direction.*
>
> *Facebook had become a tool of inspiration for me and all at once three different opportunities presented themselves. Christian Rocketeers was one of them. As I explored these three opportunities, there was a voice deep in my heart saying that I didn't need to look for purpose, God already had one for me.*
>
> *After doing the free program, Passport to Purpose, I had no doubt that working with Christian Rocketeers was where I would discover who I was in God and the purpose he had for me and my life.*
>
> *First, I have been able to build a relationship with God that is so incredible and have learned to tune in to what God is telling me and trusting his guidance. Carrie and Shawnee are both incredible women in God. They have encouraged and empowered me to foster that relationship with God.*
>
> *I have been led to start a nonprofit working with youth in foster care.*
>
> *Christian Rocketeers has provided me with a step-by-step guide on how to build a strong foundation for the nonprofit.*

Shawnee and Carrie are always there to guide and encourage me through bi-weekly coaching as well as daily support in a Facebook group. They also continue to provide opportunities and guidance in fostering my relationship with God and keeping the focus on HIM and what HE has called me to do.

The peace and joy I have found living in God's purpose is unimaginable. I would encourage anyone to step out in faith and allow Christian Rocketeers to help guide and encourage you to find and walk your purpose in God.

~ Georgia I AM ME - Empowering Teens from foster care

I would love to share all the reports we get from our clients but space will not allow. You can find a few more of them at our website ChristianRocketeers.com.

RESULTS: SHOW ME THE MONEY!

I'll bet you're thinking: one person's story is great Carrie, but I want to see results! Here are just a small sampling of the impact Christian Rocketeers has made on our and our clients nonprofits in a short time:

*In 3 hours, Dana raised $505 to purchase Bibles for her work in the Dominican Republic.

*In 3 days, Shawnee raised $3,000 for surgery expenses for a staff member.

*In 21 days, Lisa raised $7,300 through a family and friends letter to ease the hearts of hurting moms who have lost a child.
*Finding ease and grace in event planning AND raising $30,000 in a few hours to end human trafficking.

*In 2 months, we raised $42,000 to add a third floor for an education area for young moms.

*In 2 weeks, meeting an emergency funding need of $15,000 to avoid a critical piece of land deal going south.

*In a few weeks, we raised $3,000 for emergency c-section deliveries on social media alone.

*Dana was able to raise $7,000 in one day - on Giving Tuesday - for land for her educational and feeding program nonprofit.

*Early in our journey we raised over $100,000 in just six months to build a building on our new property in Kenya.

*Obtaining 16 **monthly, recurring** donors mostly through social media and conferences.

MORE THAN FINANCIAL RESULTS

In addition to funding results Christian Rocketeers clients also report:

*Bringing together active boards full of engaged members because of their work with us.

*Obtaining State Incorporation status in a matter of hours following our simple and easy steps.

*Being able to work from rest and not stress and being overwhelmed.

*Obtaining legal IRS 501(c)(3) nonprofit tax exemption status in two weeks following our simple and easy blueprint.

*Hosting events, mission trips and following all that God has for them in this life.

*Making a life saving and transforming impact all over the world:

- Feeding and educating desperate and destitute Haitian children in the Dominican Republic.
- Serving foster children through emotional and spiritual healing in after school programs on the east coast.
- Feeding and educating young children in Ghana with no other chances.
- Serving single moms in Wisconsin with second chance housing.
- Healing broken hearts of moms who lost children through conferences, wellness, and life coaching throughout the country and world!

And so much more!

HOW DO WE DO IT WITH EASE AND GRACE?

The results are endless and speak for themselves, with the ability to do this with ease and grace not stress and overwhelm! That's the most amazing part! We do all of this through our Christian Rocketeers Course, Coaching and Community.

1. **Course content**: Access to an 8 module course including: short videos, worksheets, and a ton of plug and play templates for funding, legal documents and so much more. One-year access to review the instructions and templates as much as you need while you grow your nonprofit.

Modules include: State legal documents, IRS and other legal documents, Getting Organized, Social Media, Website and Branding, Effective Fundraising, Overcome Fear of the Ask for Money, and so much more.

2. **Live Group Coaching:** 2 sessions per month group coaching sessions to get all of your questions answered and you help overcome YOUR specific obstacles as you encounter them.

3. **Community:** Access to our amazing Christian Rocketeers Master's Mind Group. You receive constant support, prayer, documents, advice, or whatever you need to help and celebrate you through tough times.

You'll also receive these special bonuses completely free.

> *All you need to get the legal process started for your nonprofit - A template to get you started on your incorporation articles, bylaws and conflict of interest policies,

> *A special mystery gift that sky-rockets your nonprofit from going in circles and hoping for money to moving forward everyday and making incredible, miraculous impact in no time.

> *The exact journaling process that has raised hundreds of thousands of dollars with ease and grace, together with templates for fundraising that will make your life simple and easy.

> *A masterclass on overcoming anxiety so you can go after your next big donation.

> *Access to a full library of training material and so much more.

YOU HAVE A CHOICE!

You can continue as you have been doing and not see the results you want and wonder if you are handling all the legal and other parts correctly. You can spend time/money searching on your own and hope for the best. But why would you want to make it harder on yourself, when we've taken all of the guesswork out for you?

To hire professionals to help you with all of this work, you would spend over $44,000 on lawyers, accountants, fundraising experts, mindset coachings and consultants. You'd be doing this on your own and you won't have a community to do it with.

Or instead, you can enroll with Christian Rocketeers for pennies on the dollar and get everything you need plus a community to surround and support you along the way!

Everything we teach in this program works in today's environment. We know because we're in the trenches everyday fundraising, managing, leading, and growing several nonprofits in the US and in Kenya ourselves.

There is no other program currently out there in the trenches with you. There is no other program I can find that is faith based and uses the Bible and God's power to help you grow your nonprofit He has called you to.

Your purchase of the Christian Rocketeers program will go to support Mercy's Light Family that you've read about throughout this book which is fighting and healing human trafficking, bringing the light of Jesus and so much more to Vipingo, Kenya.

We keep our Christian Rocketeer community small so personal attention can be given to everyone. Don't miss out on your chance to be a part of the community!

SO MUCH MORE TO SHARE
GOODBYES ARE SO HARD

I could go on for 1,000 more pages about all the amazing things God has done, taught me and shown me through this journey. Join us in our programs and we will share this ride with God and our nonprofits together! Go to www.ChristianRocketeers.com and let's get started together today! See you on the inside!

But in the meantime let me close us out in prayer!

Father God,

Thank you for doing a new thing in the heart and life of this young nonprofit leader.
Thank you for helping them live a bold and courageous life like Joshua.
Thank you that they were created to change culture like Moses.

Thank you that they have a deep love for you like David.

Thank you for raising them up to change generations to come and for such a time as this like Esther.

Thank you that they will speak with truth and clarity like Paul.

Thank you for guiding and directing them just as you did Abraham leading them to a blessing and promise for them, their families, and those that they serve.

Father, today as they take next steps in their nonprofit, remind them to release the fear and overwhelm that is holding them back. Help them to embrace all that you have ahead for them, a life that is led by your Holy Spirit and that they don't conform to the patterns of this world. Thank you that they can conquer anything that comes their way because they have the Holy Spirit living inside of them. That there is no giant too big for you and that with you nothing is impossible.

Help them to, daily, be in your Word and for their hearts and minds to be transformed. Thank you for being their perfect peace as their mind is stayed on you.

Thank you that they are created for infinitely more and that all you have ahead for them through their bold, "Here, I Am Send me" is more than they can ask, think, or imagine.

Father, pour out a blessing on their families, business, and ministry. Father, help them to daily see you at work and to take time to thank you with a grateful heart.

In Jesus Name, Amen

About the Author

"You can do this."

Carrie Reichartz, Chief Rocket Launcher of the Christian Rocketeers movement.

Her life and businesses were radically transformed 13 years ago when encountering the powerful love of God in Kenya. Shortly after receiving the honor of being a Rising Star lawyer, God interrupted her plans.

"I was called to leave my legal career and "give a voice" to women who have suffered emotional trauma including exiting of sex trafficking. I am fighting systemic spiritual, emotional, and financial poverty for young moms in Mombasa, Kenya through Operation Give Hope, the first nonprofit I established. We reach over 1,200 children each day with life changing transformation in Mombasa, Kenya."

Seeing the depth and breadth of need in the world, she created the Christian Rocketeers to train and support nonprofit and future nonprofit leaders around the globe to help them make world changing Kingdom mindset shifts that increase their capacity for the greater influence, impact, and even finances they are called to steward.

Millions of kids and adults are impacted by this work yearly!

Carrie is a wife and mother of three twenty-something children. She resides with her family just outside of Milwaukee, Wisconsin and many other places around the world.

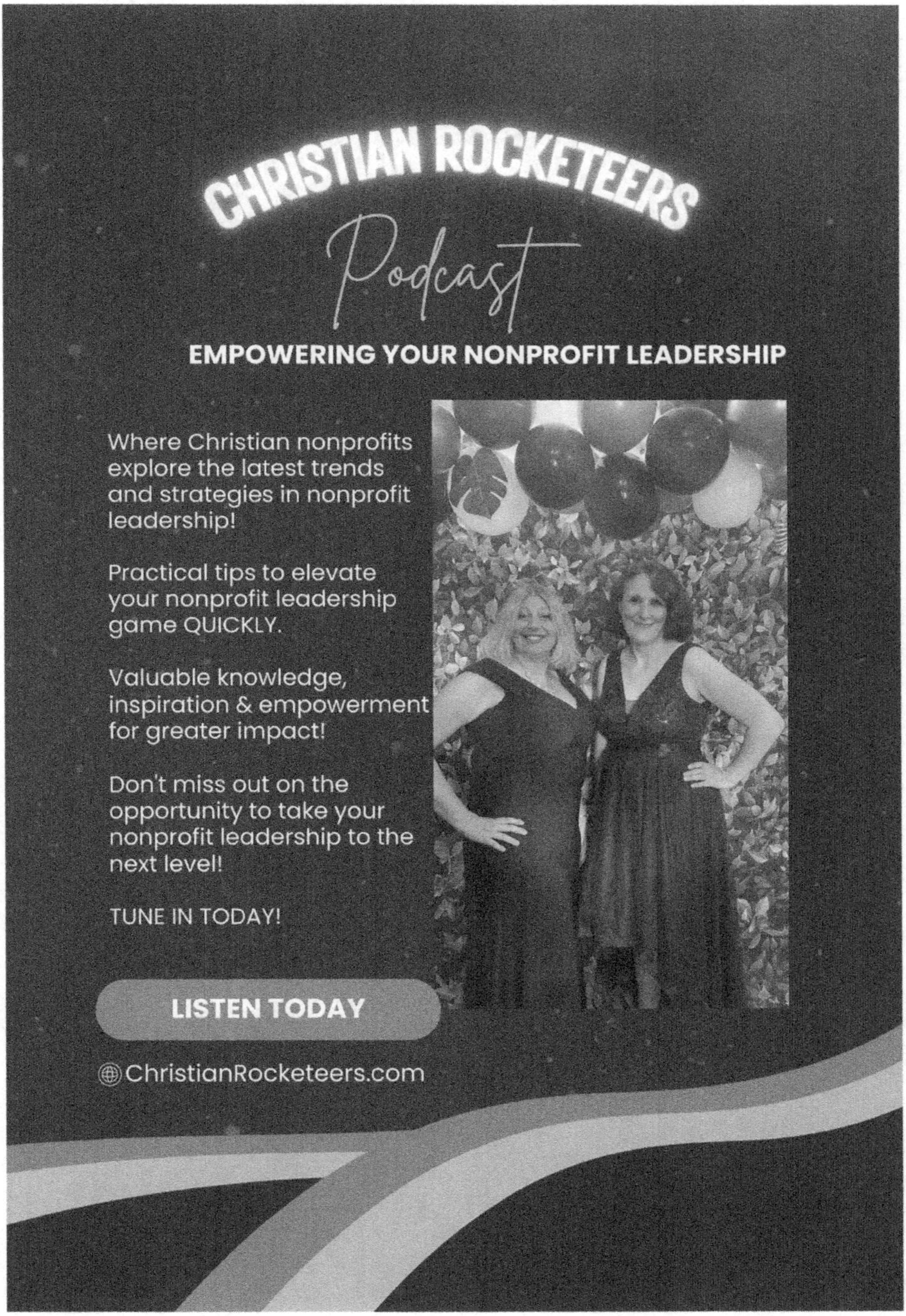
CHRISTIAN ROCKETEERS
Podcast
EMPOWERING YOUR NONPROFIT LEADERSHIP
Where Christian nonprofits explore the latest trends and strategies in nonprofit leadership!
Practical tips to elevate your nonprofit leadership game QUICKLY.
Valuable knowledge, inspiration & empowerment for greater impact!
Don't miss out on the opportunity to take your nonprofit leadership to the next level!
TUNE IN TODAY!
LISTEN TODAY
ChristianRocketeers.com

IS GOD CALLING YOU TO LAUNCH A CHRISTIAN NONPROFIT MINISTRY LIKE DANA?

➡ Dana raised $7,500 in 1 day in her Giving Tuesday campaign to raise funds for an educational and feeding center in the Dominican Republic!

➡ With Christian Rocketeers help and guidance Dana was able to revamp her "dead" board into a fully functioning in just a manner of months!

➡ Dana also reports that the organization and structure Christian Rocketeers has helped me create for my organization is amazing! Without them I lost and my systems would be a mess.

CHRISTIAN ROCKETEERS CAN HELP YOU LIKE LISA AND CHRISTINE!

Lisa and Christine from Bereaved Together, Inc. lead a nonprofit helping grieving moms and wives navigate the pain of loss and find healing and hope.

Lisa, because of using the proven Christian Rocketeers method, raised $7,500 for nonprofit in just 21 days!

YOU CAN, TOO!

LET'S START TAKING MOMENTUM BUILDING ACTION TO GROW YOUR PROFITABLE NONPROFIT MINISTRY!

ChristianRocketeers.com

OVERCOMING EMOTIONS:
30 Days in the Psalms

A Day by Day Journey to the Infinitely More Life

Grab your copy today On Amazon.com

Carrie Reichartz

OWNING YOUR STORY
So It Doesn't Own You

Want to be a better leader? Most of our decisions and reactions are on autopilot. Let's make sure we have our default settings in line!

Grab Your Copy today at ChristianRocketeers.com

Rocket Your Nonprofit

YOUR PASSPORT TO PURPOSE: 5-DAY WORLD TOUR ROCKET CHALLENGE

Find Your Purpose Today at:
ChristianRocketeers.com

Are you looking for an inspiring and empowering true story of overcoming trauma and adversity?

In this gripping memoir, Carrie Reichartz shares her journey of survival and healing after experiencing years of abuse and trauma.

With raw honesty and courage, she takes readers through the darkest moments of her life, from the fear and pain of living through sexual trauma as a child and through abusive relationships.

But this is a story of hope and resilience.
Through faith, therapy, and the support of loved ones, Reichartz learns to reclaim her life and find joy and purpose in helping others who have experienced similar trauma.

Her story is a testament to the power of the human spirit to overcome even the most difficult of circumstances.

GRAB YOUR COPY TODAY:
INFINITELYMORELIFE.ORG

FROM LAWYER TO MISSIONARY:
A JOURNEY TO KENYA AND BACK AGAIN

By Carrie Reichartz

Looking for an inspiring true story of one person's journey from a successful legal career to becoming a missionary in Kenya?

Look no further than "From Lawyer to Missionary: A Journey to Kenya" by Carrie Reichartz.

In this book, Carrie talks about how God took her from the courtroom to a mission field in Kenya. She simply said yes to a trip that was happening at her local church. However, that trip changed her life.

GRAB YOUR COPY TODAY:
INFINITELYMORELIFE.ORG

FROM LAWYER TO MISSIONARY:
THE JOURNEY CONTINUES

GRAB YOUR COPY TODAY

INFINITELYMORELIFE.ORG

Carrie Reichartz picks up where she left off in her first book, sharing her ongoing adventures as a missionary in Kenya.

Her vivid storytelling and honest reflections, Reichartz takes readers on a journey through the challenges and triumphs of her mission work.

From navigating cultural differences and language barriers to building relationships and making a difference in the lives of those she serves, Reichartz shares the highs and lows of life on the mission field.

This book is more than just a personal account, it's an invitation to join in the work of making a difference in the world.

Be a Light in THE DARKNESS

Save lives of young girls and their babies

Empower women and young moms – who have been through sexual trauma – out of poverty and into their God given purpose through discipleship, vocational & business skills!

THE NEED:

1 in every 39 women in Kenya die from pregnancy related causes.

More than 13,000 Kenyan young moms drop out of school every year due to pregnancy.

Over 500,000 illegal/unsafe abortions occur in Kenya each year.

Carrie Reichartz

Mercy's Light Family: Light In The Darkness

Where young moms, who have been sexually traumatized and are pregnant, come to find hope, love, healing, & empowerment.

Year 1

Involves extensive counseling. We focus on literacy and basic education skills.
Our goal is to teach them who they are in Christ.

Year 2

Intensive Income Capacity Building: Vocational skills in tailoring, cooking, baking, beadwork, soap mixing. Financial, educational.

Year 3

Business development. Ready to move out with their baby and support themselves.

BECOME A SPONSOR TODAY FOR ONLY $33 A MONTH!

Mercy's Light Family
P.O. Box 510376, New Berlin WI 53151
Mercyslight.org

Mercy's Light Family

Rocket Your Nonprofit

Edgar and Eve in this inspiring tale share pen pal letters back and forth. Learning about culture in the United States and Kenya using colors. Your child will learn Swahili colors and relationships through reading this story.

GET YOUR COPIES TODAY AT INFINITELYMORELIFE.ORG

Carrie Reichartz

Mercy's Light Family
GIFTS FOR A CAUSE!

Babies are being discarded in roadside ditches to die because of a dire need for education and lack of help for desperate young moms.

Put our programs change that! Purchase some items our girls make and make a huge difference!

For more Kenya items, check out Mercyslightfamily.Etsy.com

Rocket Your Nonprofit

I am Enough In Christ
Book and Bible Study

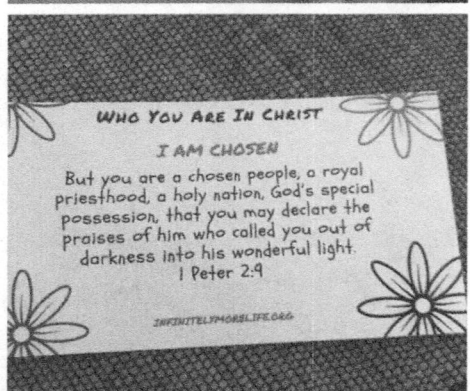

Do you desire to live an abundant life but find yourself struggling with feelings of anxiety, tiredness, depression, or overwhelm?

You are not alone. It's easy to feel like you're not enough - not smart, not pretty, not creative, not loving, etc. The *I Am Enough In Christ* Book, Workbook, and scripture cards is here to revive and empower you!

GET YOUR COPIES TODAY AT INFINITELYMORELIFE.ORG

Carrie Reichartz

Daily Encouragement

365 DAYS A YEAR....

Be encouraged, invigorated, inspired, and empowered for victory!

This daily devotional equips you to discover who you really are and revives your spirit!

With the tools and tactics provided from four different authors, you can live an abundant life every day by learning who you are in Christ.

Engaging meditative coloring exercises are included focusing on God's truth.

So be encouraged, be invigorated, be inspired, and be empowered for victory.

With this book, you'll be equipped to overcome the challenges of daily life and live in the abundance that God intended for you.

GET YOUR COPIES TODAY AT INFINITELYMORELIFE.ORG

CARLEIGH AND THE BULLIES:

Carleigh has a problem, at school girls around her make fun of her hair and clothes. She struggles going to school and believing in herself.

She meets a new friend who teaches her that it doesn't matter what the bullies say. It matters what Jesus thinks about her.

Join Carleigh and her friends as she learns the importance of knowing "Who You Are In Christ"

In this book your child will learn:
√The importance of being a true friend
√Knowing Who You are in Christ
√Building good esteem
√Helping others who are dealing with strong emotions

GET YOUR COPIES TODAY AT INFINITELYMORELIFE.ORG

Carrie Reichartz

Royalty University

LIVING THE "INFINITELY MORE LIFE" IN CHRIST

**GET YOUR COPY AT
INFINITELYMORELIFE.ORG**

ROCKET MY NONPROFIT COURSES
NONPROFIT ROCKET FUNDING BLUEPRINT
Christian Rocketeers
Passport to Funding
MINICOURSE
8 WEEK CHRISTIAN ROCKETEERS
NONPROFIT STARTUP CERTIFICATION
SIGN UP TODAY AT:
CHRISTIANROCKETEERS.COM

Follow Us on Social Media

Let's Get Connected for Our Latest News & Updates

Facebook.com/Mercyslightfamily

Instagram.com/Mercyslightfamily

Youtube.com/infinitelymorelife

Mercy's Light Family

Rocket Your Nonprofit

Christian Rocketeers

Follow Us on Social Media

FACEBOOK.COM/CHRISTIANROCKETEERS

YOUTUBE.COM/CHRISTIANROCKETEERS

INSTAGRAM.COM/CHRISTIANROCKETEERS

FACEBOOK COMMUNITY: BIT.LY/CHRISTIANROCKETEERS

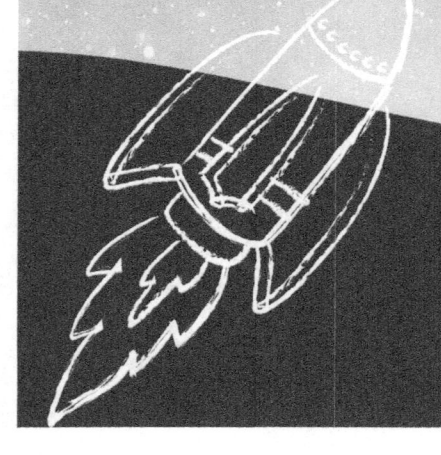

Made in the USA
Monee, IL
29 February 2024

54244924R00095